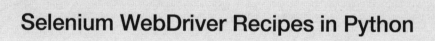

Selenium WebDriver Recipes in Python

The problem solving guide to Selenium WebDriver

Zhimin Zhan

Selenium WebDriver Recipes in Python

The problem solving guide to Selenium WebDriver

Zhimin Zhan

ISBN 978-1-51-425657-2

Contents

Preface

After observing many failed test automation attempts by using expensive commercial test automation tools, I am delighted to see that the value of open-source testing frameworks has finally been recognized. I still remember the day (a rainy day at a Gold Coast hotel in 2011) when I found out that the Selenium WebDriver was the most wanted testing skill in terms of the number of job ads on the Australia's top job-seeking site.

Now Selenium WebDriver is big in the testing world. We all know software giants such as Facebook and LinkedIn use it, immensely-comprehensive automated UI testing enables them pushing out releases several times a day[1]. However, from my observation, many software projects, while using Selenium, are not getting much value from test automation, and certainly nowhere near its potential. A clear sign of this is that the regression testing is not conducted on a daily basis (if test automation is done well, it will happen naturally).

Among the factors contributing to test automation failures, a key one is that automation testers lack sufficient knowledge in the test framework. It is quite common to see some testers or developers get excited when they first create a few simple test cases and see them run in a browser. However, it doesn't take long for them to encounter some obstacles: such as being unable to automate certain operations. If one step cannot be automated, the whole test case does not work, which is the nature of test automation. Searching solutions online is not always successful, and posting questions on forums and waiting can be frustrating (usually, very few people seek professional help from test automation coaches). Not surprisingly, many projects eventually gave up test automation or just used it for testing a handful of scenarios.

The motivation of this book is to help motivated testers work better with Selenium. The book contains over 150 recipes for web application tests with Selenium. If you have read one of my other books: *Practical Web Test Automation*[2], you probably know my style: practical. I will let the test scripts do most of the talking. These recipe test scripts are 'live', as I have created the target test site and included offline test web pages. With both, you can:

1. **Identify** your issue
2. **Find** the recipe
3. **Run** the test case
4. **See** test execution in your browser

---

[1]http://www.wired.com/business/2013/04/linkedin-software-revolution/
[2]https://leanpub.com/practical-web-test-automation

Who should read this book

This book is for testers or programmers who are writing (or want to learn) automated tests with Selenium WebDriver. In order to get the most of this book, basic Ruby coding skill is required.

How to read this book

Usually, a 'recipe' book is a reference book. Readers can go directly to the part that interests them. For example, if you are testing a multiple select list and don't know how, you can look up in the Table of Contents, then go to the chapter. This book supports this style of reading. Since the recipes are arranged according to their levels of complexity, readers will also be able to work through the book from the front to back if they are looking to learn test automation with Selenium.

Recipe test scripts

To help readers to learn more effectively, this book has a dedicated site[3] which contains the sample test scripts and related resources.

As an old saying goes, "There's more than one way to skin a cat." You can achieve the same testing outcome with test scripts implemented in different ways. The recipe test scripts in this book are written for simplicity, there is always room for improvement. But for many, to understand the solution quickly and get the job done are probably more important.

If you have a better and simpler way, please let me know.

All recipe test scripts are Selenium 2 (aka Selenium WebDriver WebDriver) compliant, and can be run on Firefox, Chrome and Internet Explorer on multiple platforms. I plan to keep the test scripts updated with the latest stable Selenium version.

Send me feedback

I would appreciate your comments, suggestions, reports on errors in the book and the recipe test scripts. You may submit your feedback on the book's site.

Zhimin Zhan

March 2015

---

[3]http://zhimin.com/books/selenium-recipes

1. Introduction

Selenium is a free and open source library for automated testing web applications. I assume that you have had some knowledge of Selenium, based on the fact that you picked up this book (or opened it in your eBook reader).

1.1 Selenium

Selenium was originally created in 2004 by Jason Huggins, who was later joined by his other ThoughtWorks colleagues. Selenium supports all major browsers and tests can be written in many programming languages and run on Windows, Linux and Macintosh platforms.

Selenium 2 is merged with another test framework WebDriver (that's why you see 'selenium-webdriver') led by Simon Stewart at Google (update: Simon now works at FaceBook), Selenium 2.0 was released in July 2011.

1.2 Selenium language bindings

Selenium tests can be written in multiple programming languages such as Java, C#, Python, JavaScript and Ruby (the core ones). Quite commonly, I heard the saying such as *"This is a Java project, so we shall write tests in Java as well"*. I disagree. Software testing is to verify whether programmer's work meets customer's needs. In a sense, testers are representing customers. Testers should have more weight on deciding the test syntax than programmers. Plus, why would you mandate that your testers should have the same programming language skills as the programmers. In my subjective view, scripting languages such as Ruby and Python are more suitable for test scripts than compiled languages such as C# and Java (Confession: I have been programming in Java for over 10 years). By the way, we call them test scripts, for a reason.

All examples in this book are written in Selenium with Ruby binding. This does not mean this book is limited to testers/developers who know Ruby. As you will see the examples below, the use of Selenium in different bindings are very similar. Once you master one, you can apply it to others quite easily. Take a look at a simple Selenium test script in five different language bindings: Java, C#, JavaScript, Ruby and Python.

Java:

```
import org.openqa.selenium.By;
import org.openqa.selenium.WebDriver;
import org.openqa.selenium.WebElement;
import org.openqa.selenium.firefox.FirefoxDriver;

public class GoogleSearch  {
  public static void main(String[] args) {
    // Create a new instance of the html unit driver
    // Notice that the remainder of the code relies on the interface,
    // not the implementation.
    WebDriver driver = new FirefoxDriver();

    // And now use this to visit Google
    driver.get("http://www.google.com");

    // Find the text input element by its name
    WebElement element = driver.findElement(By.name("q"));

    // Enter something to search for
    element.sendKeys("Hello Selenium WebDriver!");

    // Submit the form based on an element in the form
    element.submit();

    // Check the title of the page
    System.out.println("Page title is: " + driver.getTitle());
  }
}
```

C#:

```
using System;
using OpenQA.Selenium;
using OpenQA.Selenium.Firefox;
using OpenQA.Selenium.Support.UI;

class GoogleSearch
{
  static void Main()
  {
    IWebDriver driver = new FirefoxDriver();
    driver.Navigate().GoToUrl("http://www.google.com");
    IWebElement query = driver.FindElement(By.Name("q"));
    query.SendKeys("Hello Selenium WebDriver!");
    query.Submit();
    Console.WriteLine(driver.Title);
  }
}
```

JavaScript:

```
var webdriver = require('selenium-webdriver');
var driver = new webdriver.Builder()
    .forBrowser('chrome')
    .build();

driver.get('http://www.google.com/ncr');
driver.findElement(webdriver.By.name('q')).sendKeys('webdriver');
driver.findElement(webdriver.By.name('btnG')).click();
driver.wait(webdriver.until.titleIs('webdriver - Google Search'), 1000);
console.log(driver.title);
```

Ruby:

```
require "selenium-webdriver"

driver = Selenium::WebDriver.for :firefox
driver.navigate.to "http://www.google.com"

element = driver.find_element(:name, 'q')
element.send_keys "Hello Selenium WebDriver!"
element.submit

puts driver.title
```

Python:

```
from selenium import webdriver

driver = webdriver.Firefox()
driver.get("http://www.google.com")

elem = driver.find_element_by_name("q")
elem.send_keys("Hello WebDriver!")
elem.submit()

print(driver.title)
```

1.3 Install Selenium Python

1. Download and install Python.

   Python 2 is pre-installed on Mac and most Linux distributions. For new Python projects, I would recommend Python 3, which was first released in 2008. Here are the instructions to install Python on Windows.

   Download latest installer[1] and run the installer.

---

[1]https://www.python.org/downloads

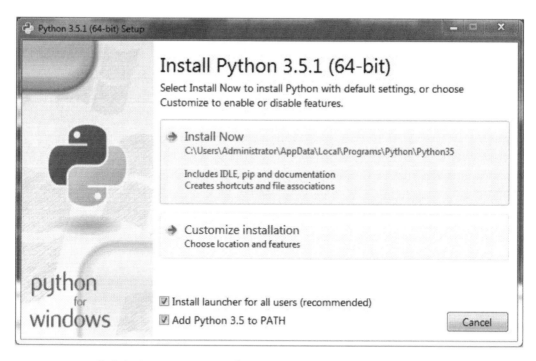

Accept all default options except "Add python.exe to Path" for convenience.

For Mac,

```
brew install python3
```

2. Install Selenium-WebDriver for Python.

PIP is the package manager for Python. PIP comes with Python installer, run the command below to upgrade to the latest PIP version.

```
> python -m pip install --upgrade pip
```

Install Selenium-WebDriver for Python.

```
C:\Users\Administrator>pip3 install selenium
Collecting selenium
  Downloading selenium-3.0.2-py2.py3-none-any.whl (915kB)
    100% |################################| 921kB 525kB/s
  Installing collected packages: selenium
  Successfully installed selenium-3.0.2
```

3. Your target browses are installed, such as Chrome and Firefox.

Now you are ready to run Selenium script. Type in the above python script (*google search*) in a text editor such as NotePad and save as "google_search.py". Run the command below in a command window.

```
> py google_search.py
```

You will see Firefox browser starting up and performing a Google search.

1.4 Cross browser testing

The biggest advantage of Selenium over other web test frameworks, in my opinion, is that it supports all major web browsers: Firefox, Chrome and Internet Explorer. The browser market nowadays is more diversified (based on the StatsCounter[2], the usage share in April 2017 for Chrome, IE/Edge and Firefox are 63.36%, 12.94% and 14.17% respectively). It is logical that all external facing web sites require serious cross-browser testing. Selenium is a natural choice for this purpose, as it far exceeds other commercial tools and open-source test frameworks.

Firefox

Firefox (up to v46[3]) comes with WebDriver support. geckodriver[4] is required for Firefox 47+.

The test script below (in a file named: *ch01_open_firefox.py*) will open a web site in a new Firefox window.

---

[2]http://en.wikipedia.org/wiki/Usage_share_of_web_browsers

[3]https://download-installer.cdn.mozilla.net/pub/firefox/releases/46.0.1/

[4]https://github.com/mozilla/geckodriver/releases/

```
from selenium import webdriver
driver = webdriver.Firefox()
driver.get("http://testwisely.com/demo")
```

Chrome

To run Selenium tests in Google Chrome, besides the Chrome browser itself, *ChromeDriver* needs to be installed.

Installing ChromeDriver is easy: go to ChromeDriver site[5].

Index of /2.29/

Name	Last modified	Size	ETag
Parent Directory			
chromedriver_linux32.zip	2017-04-04 04:18:24	3.28MB	ba8f027f85b60ba5b46d3913f8135ec2
chromedriver_linux64.zip	2017-04-04 01:21:21	3.24MB	06a3f9c57ced2e3ea4e7f3ec258b3957
chromedriver_mac64.zip	2017-04-04 05:55:53	4.63MB	5d71bc70834c2ad8a7baf7a901d53566
chromedriver_win32.zip	2017-04-04 05:29:10	3.62MB	b6e3a3fa31d2b45e482b44dcf8abd833
notes.txt	2017-04-04 16:00:57	0.01MB	f31bb0b18e17e774f33cef84ad03e9b6

Download the one for your target platform, unzip it and put **chromedriver** executable in your PATH. To verify the installation, open a command window (terminal for Unix/Mac), execute command *chromedriver,* You shall see:

```
C:\>chromedriver
Starting ChromeDriver 2.29.461591 (62ebf098771772160f391d75e589dc567915b233) on port 9515
Only local connections are allowed.
```

The test script below opens a site in a new Chrome browser window and closes it one second later.

---

[5]https://sites.google.com/a/chromium.org/chromedriver/downloads

```
from selenium import webdriver
import time

driver = webdriver.Chrome()
driver.get("http://testwisely.com/demo")
time.sleep(1)
driver.quit()
```

Internet Explorer

Selenium requires IEDriverServer to drive IE browser. Its installation process is very similar to *ChromeDriver*. IEDriverServer is available at http://www.seleniumhq.org/download/[6]. Choose the right one based on your windows version (32 or 64 bit).

> Download version 3.4 for (recommended) 32 bit Windows IE or 64 bit Windows IE
> CHANGELOG

When a tests starts to execute in IE, before navigating the target test site, you will see this first:

Depending on the version of IE, configurations may be required. Please see IE and IEDriverServer Runtime Configuration[7] for details.

```
from selenium import webdriver
driver = webdriver.Ie()
driver.get("http://testwisely.com/demo")
```

Edge

Edge is Microsoft's new and default web browser on Windows 10. To drive Edge with WebDriver, you need download Microsoft WebDriver[8]. After installation, you will find the executable (*MicrosoftWebDriver.exe*) under *Program Files* folder, add it to your PATH.

---

[6]http://www.seleniumhq.org/download/
[7]https://code.google.com/p/selenium/wiki/InternetExplorerDriver#Required_Configuration
[8]https://developer.microsoft.com/en-us/microsoft-edge/tools/webdriver/

However, I couldn't get it working after installing a new version of Microsoft WebDriver. One workaround is to specify the driver path in test scripts specifically:

```python
from selenium import webdriver
import time
import os


# copy MicrosoftWebDriver.exe to the test script directory
dir = os.path.dirname(__file__)
edge_path = dir + "\MicrosoftWebDriver.exe"
driver = webdriver.Edge(edge_path)
driver.get("http://testwisely.com/demo")
```

1.5 unittest - Python Unit Testing Framework

Selenium drives browsers. However, to make the effective use of Selenium scripts for testing, we need to put them in a test framework that defines test structures and provides assertions (performing checks in test scripts). In this book, I use *unittest*, also known as "PyUnit", the unit testing framework for Python. Here is an example.

```python
import unittest
from selenium import webdriver

class FooBarTestCase(unittest.TestCase):

  @classmethod
  def setUpClass(cls):
    cls.driver = webdriver.Chrome()

  @classmethod
  def tearDownClass(cls):
    cls.driver.quit()

  def setUp(self):
    self.driver.get("http://travel.agileway.net")

  def tearDown(self):
```

```
      self.driver.find_element_by_link_text("Sign off").click()

  def test_first_case(self):
    self.assertEqual("Agile Travel", self.driver.title)
    self.driver.find_element_by_name("username").send_keys("agileway")
    # ...

  def test_second_case(self):
    self.driver.find_element_by_id("register_link").click()
    # ...
    self.assertIn("Register", self.driver.find_element_by_tag_name("body").t\
ext)
```

The keywords class, `setUpClass, setUp and def test_xxx` define the structure of a test script file.

- **class FooBarTestCase(unittest.TestCase):**

  Test suite name for grouping related test cases.
- **setUpClass()** and **tearDownClass()**.

  Optional test statements run before and after all test cases, typically starting a new browser window in setupClass and close it in tearDownClass.
- **setUp()** and **tearDown()**.

  Optional test statements run before and after each test case.
- **def test_xxx(self):**

  Individual test cases.
- **Assertions**

  assertEqual() and assertIn are PyUnit's two assertion methods which are used to perform checks. More assert methods[9]

You will find more about unittest from its home page[10]. However, I honestly don't think it is necessary. The part used for test scripts is not much and quite intuitive. After studying and trying out some examples, you will be quite comfortable with it.

---

[9]https://docs.python.org/3/library/unittest.html#assert-methods
[10]https://docs.python.org/3/library/unittest.html

1.6 Run recipe scripts

Test scripts for all recipes can be downloaded from the book site. They are all in ready-to-run state. I include the target web pages/sites as well as Selenium test scripts. There are two kinds of target web pages: local HTML files and web pages on a live site. Running tests written for a live site requires Internet connection.

Run tests in PyCharm IDE

The most convenient way to run one test case or a test suite is to do it in an IDE, such as PyCharm.

 When you have a large number of test cases, then the most effective way to run all tests is done by a Continuous Integration process.

Find the test case

You can locate the recipe either by following the chapter or searching by name. There are over 150 test cases in the recipes test project. Here is the quickest way to find the one you want in PyCharm.

Select menu 'Navigation' → 'Go to Symbol ...'.

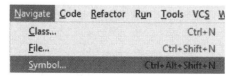

A pop up window lists all test cases in the project for your selection. The finding starts as soon as you type.

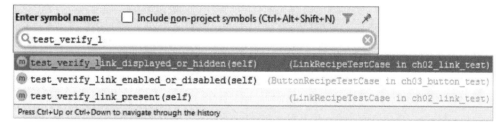

Run individual test case

Move mouse to a line within a test case (starting `def test_xxx)(self):`). Right click and select "Run 'Unittest test_xxx'" to run this case.

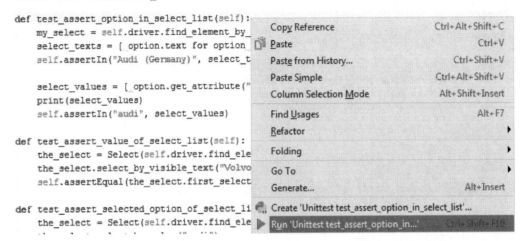

The below is a screenshot of execution panel when one test case failed,

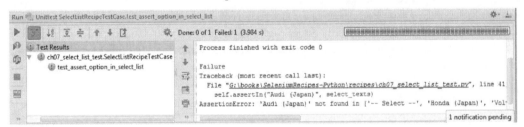

Run all test cases in a test script file

You can also run all test cases in a test script file by right clicking the file name in the project pane and select "Run 'Unittests in test_file.py'".

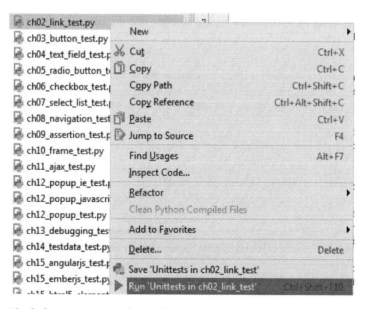

The below is a screenshot of the execution panel when all test cases in a test script file passed,

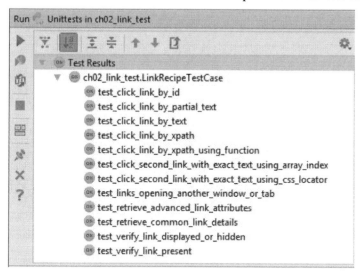

Run tests from command line

One advantage of open-source test frameworks, such as Selenium, is FREEDOM. You can edit the test scripts in any text editors and run them from a command line.

To run test cases in a test script file (named google_test.py), enter command

```
> python -m unittest google_test.py
```

Run multiple test script files in one go:

```
> python -m unittest first_test.py  second_test.py
```

The command syntax is identical for Mac OS X and Linux platforms.

2. Locating web elements

As you might have already figured out, to drive an element in a page, we need to find it first. Selenium uses what is called locators to find and match the elements on web page. There are 8 locators in Selenium:

Locator	Example
ID	`find_element_by_id("user")`
Name	`find_element_by_name("username")`
Link Text	`find_element_by_link_text("Login")`
Partial Link Text	`find_element_by_partial_link_text("Next")`
XPath	`find_element_by_xpath("//div[@id="login"]/input")`
Tag Name	`find_element_by_tag_name("body")`
Class Name	`find_element_by_class_name("table")`
CSS	`find_element_by_css_selector("#login > input[type="text"]")`

You may use any one of them to narrow down the element you are looking for.

2.1 Start browser

Testing websites starts with a browser. The test script below launches a Firefox browser window and navigate to a site.

```
from selenium import webdriver
driver = webdriver.Firefox()
driver.get("http://testwisely.com/demo")
```

Use `webdriver.Chrome` and `webdriver.Ie()` for testing in Chrome and IE respectively.

Test Pages

I prepared the test pages for the recipes, you can download them (in a zip file) at the book's site[a]. Unzip to a local directory and refer to test pages like this:

```
import urllib
# ...
site_path = os.path.dirname(os.path.realpath(__file__)) + "/../site"
site_url  = urllib.request.pathname2url(site_path)

driver.get(site_url + "/locators.html")

__file__ is the directory where the test script is.
```
ᵃhttp://zhimin.com/books/selenium-recipes-python

I recommend, for beginners, to close the browser window at the end of a test case.

```
driver.quit
```

2.2 Find element by ID

Using IDs is the easiest and the safest way to locate an element in HTML. If the page is W3C HTML conformed[1], the IDs should be unique and identified in web controls. In comparison to texts, test scripts that use IDs are less prone to application changes (e.g. developers may decide to change the label, but are less likely to change the ID).

```
driver.find_element_by_id("submit_btn").click    # Button
driver.find_element_by_id("cancel_link").click   # Link
driver.find_element_by_id("username").send_keys("agileway")  # Textfield
driver.find_element_by_id("alert_div").text      # HTML Div element
```

2.3 Find element by Name

The name attributes are used in form controls such as text fields and radio buttons. The values of the name attributes are passed to the server when a form is submitted. In terms of least likelihood of a change, the name attribute is probably only second to ID.

[1]http://www.w3.org/TR/WCAG20-TECHS/H93.html

```
driver.find_element_by_name("comment").send_keys("Selenium Cool")
```

2.4 Find element by Link Text

For Hyperlinks only. Using a link's text is probably the most direct way to click a link, as it is what we see on the page.

```
driver.find_element_by_link_text("Cancel").click
```

2.5 Find element by Partial Link Text

Selenium allows you to identify a hyperlink control with a partial text. This can be quite useful when the text is dynamically generated. In other words, the text on one web page might be different on your next visit. We might be able to use the common text shared by these dynamically generated link texts to identify them.

```
# will click the "Cancel" link
driver.find_element_by_partial_link_text("ance").click
```

2.6 Find element by XPath

XPath, the XML Path Language, is a query language for selecting nodes from an XML document. When a browser renders a web page, it parses it into a DOM tree or similar. XPath can be used to refer a certain node in the DOM tree. If this sounds a little too much technical for you, don't worry, just remember XPath is the most powerful way to find a specific web control.

```
# clicking the checkbox under 'div2' container
driver.find_element_by_xpath("//*[@id='div2']/input[@type='checkbox']").clic\
k()
```

Some testers feel intimidated by the complexity of XPath. However, in practice, there is only limited scope of XPath to master for testers.

Avoid using copied XPath from Browser's Developer Tool

Browser's Developer Tool (right click to select 'Inspect element' to show) is very useful for identifying a web element in web page. You may get the XPath of a web element there, as shown below (in Chrome):

The copied XPath for the second "Click here" link in the example:

```
//*[@id="container"]/div[3]/div[2]/a
```

It works. However, I do not recommend this approach as the test script is fragile. If developer adds another div under <div id='container'>, the copied XPath is no longer correct for the element while //div[contains(text(), "Second")]/a[text()="Click here"] still works.

In summary, XPath is a very powerful way to locating web elements when by_id, by_name or by_link_text are not applicable. Try to use a XPath expression that is less vulnerable to structure changes around the web element.

2.7 Find element by Tag Name

There are a limited set of tag names in HTML. In other words, many elements share the same tag names on a web page. We normally don't use the tag_name locator by itself to locate an element. We often use it with others in a chained locators (see the section below). However, there is an exception.

```
driver.find_element_by_tag_name("body").text
```

The above test statement returns the text view of a web page. This is a very useful one as Selenium WebDriver does not have built-in method to return the text of a web page.

2.8 Find element by Class Name

The class attribute of a HTML element is used for styling. It can also be used for identifying elements. Commonly, a HTML element's class attribute has multiple values, like below.

```
<a href="back.html" class="btn btn-default">Cancel</a>
<input type="submit" class="btn btn-deault btn-primary">Submit</input>
```

You may use any one of them.

```
driver.find_element_by_class_name("btn-primary").click()   # Submit button
driver.find_element_by_class_name("btn").click()           # Cancel link

# the below will return error "Compound class names not permitted"
# driver.find_element_by_class_name("btn btn-deault btn-primary").click()
```

The class_name locator is convenient for testing JavaScript/CSS libraries (such as TinyMCE) which typically use a set of defined class names.

```
# inline editing
driver.find_element_by_id("client_notes").click()
time.sleep(0.5)
driver.find_element_by_class_name("editable-textarea").send_keys("inline not\
es")
time.sleep(0.5)
driver.find_element_by_class_name("editable-submit").click()
```

2.9 Find element by CSS Selector

You may also use CSS Path to locate a web element.

```
driver.find_element_by_css_selector("#div2 > input[type='checkbox']").click()
```

However, the use of CSS selector is generally more prone to structure changes of a web page.

2.10 Chain find_element to find child elements

For a page containing more than one elements with the same attributes, like the one below, we could use XPath locator.

```
<div id="div1">
  <input type="checkbox" name="same" value="on"> Same checkbox in Div 1
</div>
<div id="div2">
  <input type="checkbox" name="same" value="on"> Same checkbox in Div 2
</div>
```

There is another way: chain find_element to find a child element.

```
driver.find_element_by_id("div2").find_element_by_name("same").click()
```

2.11 Find multiple elements

As its name suggests, find_elements return a list of matched elements. Its syntax is exactly the same as find_element, i.e. can use any of 8 locators.

The test statements will find two checkboxes under div#container and click the second one.

```
checkbox_elems = driver.find_elements_by_xpath("//div[@id='container']//inpu\
t[@type='checkbox']")
print(len(checkbox_elems))   # => 2
checkbox_elems[1].click()
```

Sometimes find_element fails due to multiple matching elements on a page, which you were not aware of. find_elements will come in handy to find them out.

3. Hyperlink

Hyperlinks (or links) are fundamental elements of web pages. As a matter of fact, it is hyperlinks that makes the World Wide Web possible. A sample link is provided below, along with the HTML source.

Recommend Selenium

HTML Source

```
<a href="index.html" id="recommend_selenium_link" class="nav" data-id="123" \
style="font-size: 14px;">Recommend Selenium</a>
```

3.1 Start browser

Testing web sites starts with a browser.

```
from selenium import webdriver
driver  = webdriver.Firefox()
driver.get("http://testwisely.com/demo")
```

Use `webdriver.Chrome()` and `webdriver.Ie()` for testing in Chrome and IE respectively.

I recommend, for beginners, closing the browser window at the end of a test case.

```
driver.quit()
```

3.2 Click a link by text

Using text is probably the most direct way to click a link in Selenium, as it is what we see on the page.

```
driver.find_element_by_link_text("Recommend Selenium").click()
```

A Note for testers coming from Ruby

In Ruby, round brackets ( ) is optional when calling a function.

```
driver.find_element(:link_text, "Register").click    # OK
```

However, the below test script won't work in Python.

```
driver.find_element_by_link_text("Register").click    # wrong
driver.find_element_by_link_text("Register").click()  # correct
```

This syntax issue is not a problem if it throws an error, but it does not. This test statement will execute, but not clicking the link!

3.3 Click a link by ID

```
driver.find_element_by_id("recommend_selenium_link").click()
```

Furthermore, if you are testing a web site with multiple languages, using IDs is probably the only feasible option. You do not want to write test scripts like below:

```
if is_italian?
  driver.find_element_by_link_text("Accedi").click
elsif is_chinese?  # a helper function determines the locale
  driver.find_element_by_link_text("登录").click
else
  driver.find_element_by_link_text("Sign in").click
end
```

3.4 Click a link by partial text

```
driver.find_element_by_partial_link_text("partial").click()
```

3.5 Click a link by XPath

The example below is finding a link with text 'Recommend Selenium' under a ‹p› tag.

```
driver.find_element_by_xpath("//p/a[text()='Recommend Selenium']").click()
```

Your might say the example before (find by :link_text) is simpler and more intuitive, that's correct. but let's examine another example:

First div Click here
Second div Click here

On this page, there are two 'Click here' links.

HTML Source

```
<div>
  First div
  <a href="link-url.html">Click here</a>
</div>
<div>
  Second div
  <a href="link-partial.html">Click here</a>
</div>
```

If a test case requires you to click the second 'Click here' link, the simple find_element_by_-link_text('Click here') won't work (as it clicks the first one). Here is a way to accomplish using XPath:

```
driver.find_element_by_xpath('//div[contains(text(), "Second")]/a[text()="Cl\
ick here"]').click()
```

3.6 Click Nth link with exact same label

It is not uncommon that there are more than one link with exactly the same text. By default, Selenium will choose the first one. What if you want to click the second or Nth one?

The web page below contains three 'Show Answer" links,

1. Do you think automated testing is important and valuable? Show Answer

2. Why didn't you do automated testing in your projects previously? Show Answer

3. Your project now has so comprehensive automated test suite, What changed? Show Answer

To click the second one,

```
driver.find_elements_by_link_text("Show Answer")[1].click() # second link
```

find_elements_xxx return a list (also called array) of web controls matching the criteria in appearing order. Selenium (in fact Python) uses 0-based indexing, i.e., the first one is 0.

3.7 Click Nth link by CSS

You may also use CSS Path to locate a web element.

```
# the 3rd link
driver.find_element_by_css_selector("p > a:nth-child(3)").click()
```

However, generally speaking, the use of stylesheet is more prone to changes.

3.8 Verify a link present or not?

```
assertTrue(driver.find_element_by_link_text("Recommend Selenium").is_display\
ed())
driver.find_element_by_link_text("Hide").click()
time.sleep(1) # delay 1 second
driver.find_element_by_link_text("Hide").click()
try:
  # different from Watir, selenium returns element not found if hidden
  # the below will throw NoSuchElementException
  self.assertFalse(driver.find_element_by_link_text("Recommend Selenium").is\
_displayed())
except:
  print("[Selenium] The hidden link cannot be found")

driver.find_element_by_link_text("Show").click()
time.sleep(1)
self.assertTrue(driver.find_element_by_link_text("Recommend Selenium").is_di\
splayed())
```

3.9 Getting link data attributes

Once a web control is identified, we can get its other attributes of the element. This is generally applicable to most of the controls.

```
assertIn("/site/index.html", driver.find_element_by_link_text("Recommend Sel\
enium").get_attribute("href"))
assertEqual(driver.find_element_by_link_text("Recommend Selenium").get_attri\
bute("id"), "recommend_selenium_link")
assertEqual(driver.find_element_by_id("recommend_selenium_link").text, "Reco\
mmend Selenium")
assertEqual(driver.find_element_by_id("recommend_selenium_link").tag_name, "\
a")
```

Also you can get the value of custom attributes of this element and its inline CSS style.

```
assertEqual(driver.find_element_by_id("recommend_selenium_link").get_attribu\
te("style"), "font-size: 14px;")
assertEqual(driver.find_element_by_id("recommend_selenium_link").get_attribu\
te("data-id"), "123")
```

3.10 Test links open a new browser window

Clicking the link below will open the linked URL in a new browser window or tab.

```
<a href="http://testwisely.com/demo" target="_blank">Open new window</a>
```

While we could use switch_to method (see chapter 10) to find the new browser window, it will be easier to perform all testing within one browser window. Here is how:

```
current_url = driver.current_url
new_window_url = driver.find_element_by_link_text("Open new window").get_att\
ribute("href")
driver.get(new_window_url)
# ... testing on new site
driver.find_element_by_name("name").send_keys("sometext")
driver.get(current_url) # back
```

In this test script, we use a local variable (a programming term) 'current_url' to store the current URL.

4. Button

Buttons can come in two forms - standard and submit buttons. Standard buttons are usually created by the 'button' tag, whereas submit buttons are created by the 'input' tag (normally within form controls).

Standard button

[Choose Selenium]

Submit button in a form

Username: [_____] [Submit]

HTML Source

```
<button id="selenium_btn" class="nav" data-id="123" style="font-size: 14px;"\
>Choose Selenium</button>
<!-- ... -->
<form name="input" action="index.html" method="get">
  Username: <input type="text" name="user">
  <input type="submit" name="submit_action" value="Submit">
</form>
```

Please note that some controls look like buttons, but are actually hyperlinks by CSS styling.

4.1 Click a button by text

```
driver.find_element_by_xpath("//button[contains(text(),'Choose Selenium')]")\
.click()
```

4.2 Click a form button by text

For an input button (in a HTML input tag) in a form, the text shown on the button is the 'value' attribute which might contain extra spaces or invisible characters.

```
<input type="submit" name="submit_action" value="Space After "/>
```

The test script below will fail as there is a space character in the end.

```
driver.find_element_by_xpath("//input[@value='Space After']").click()
```

Changing to match the value exactly will fix it.

```
driver.find_element_by_xpath("//input[@value='Space After ']").click()
```

4.3 Submit a form

In the official Selenium tutorial, the operation of clicking a form submit button is done by calling *submit* function on an input element within a form. For example, the test script below is to test user sign in.

```
username_element = driver.find_element_by_name("user")
username_element.send_keys("agileway")
password_element = driver.find_element_by_name("password")
password_element.send_keys("secret")
username_element.submit()
```

However, this is not my preferred approach. Whenever possible, I write test scripts this way: one test step corresponds to one user operation, such as a text entry or a mouse click. This helps me to identify issues quicker during test debugging. Using *submit* means testers need a step to define a variable to store an identified element (line 1 in above test script), to me, it breaks the flow. Here is my version:

```
driver.find_element_by_name("user").send_keys("agileway")
driver.find_element_by_name("password").send_keys("secret")
driver.find_element_by_xpath("//input[@value='Sign in']").click()
```

Furthermore, if there is more than one submit button (unlikely but possible) in a form, calling *submit* is equivalent to clicking the first submit button only, which might cause confusion.

4.4 Click a button by ID

As always, a better way to identify a button is to use IDs. This applies to all controls, if there are IDs present.

```
driver.find_element_by_id("choose_selenium_btn").click()
```

 For testers who work with the development team, rather than spending hours finding a way to identify a web control, just go to programmers and ask them to add IDs. It usually takes very little effort for programmers to do so.

4.5 Click a button by name

In an input button, we can use a new generic attribute name to locate a control.

```
driver.find_element_by_name("submit_action").click()
```

4.6 Click a image button

There is also another type of 'button': an image that works like a submit button in a form.

```
<input type="image" src="images/button_go.jpg"/>
```

Besides using ID, the button can also be identified by using *src* attribute.

```
driver.find_element_by_xpath("//input[contains(@src, 'button_go.jpg')]").cli\
ck()
```

4.7 Click a button via JavaScript

You may also invoke clicking a button via JavaScript. I had a case where normal approaches didn't click a button reliably on Firefox, but this JavaScript way worked well.

```
the_btn = driver.find_element_by_id("searchBtn")
driver.execute_script("arguments[0].click();", the_btn);
```

4.8 Assert a button present

Just like hyperlinks, we can use displayed? to check whether a control is present on a web page. This check applies to most of the web controls in Selenium.

```
assertTrue(driver.find_element_by_id("choose_selenium_btn").is_displayed())
driver.find_element_by_link_text("Hide").click()
time.sleep(0.5)
assertFalse(driver.find_element_by_id("choose_selenium_btn").is_displayed())
```

4.9 Assert a button enabled or disabled?

A web control can be in a disabled state. A disabled button is un-clickable, and it is displayed differently.

Normally enabling or disabling buttons (or other web controls) is triggered by JavaScripts.

```
assertTrue(driver.find_element_by_id("choose_selenium_btn").is_enabled())
driver.find_element_by_link_text("Disable").click()
time.sleep(0.5)
assertFalse(driver.find_element_by_id("choose_selenium_btn").is_enabled())
driver.find_element_by_link_text("Enable").click()
time.sleep(0.5)
assertTrue(driver.find_element_by_id("choose_selenium_btn").is_enabled())
```

5. TextField and TextArea

Text fields are commonly used in a form to pass user entered text data to the server. There are two variants (prior to HTML5): password fields and text areas. The characters in password fields are masked (shown as asterisks or circles). Text areas allows multiple lines of texts.

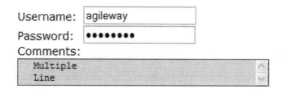

HTML Source

```
Username: <input type="text" name="username" id="user"><br>
Password: <input type="password" name="password" id="pass"> <br/>
Comments: <br/>
<textarea id="comments" rows="2" cols="60" name="comments"></textarea>
```

5.1 Enter text into a text field by name

```
driver.find_element_by_name("username").send_keys("agileway")
```

The 'name' attribute is the identification used by the programmers to process data. It applies to all the web controls in a standard web form.

5.2 Enter text into a text field by ID

```
driver.find_element_by_id("user").send_keys("tester1")
```

5.3 Enter text into a password field

In Selenium, password text fields are treated as normal text fields, except that the entered text is masked.

```
driver.find_element_by_id("pass").send_keys("testisfun")
```

5.4 Clear a text field

Calling `send_keys` to the same text field will concatenate the new text with the old text. So it is a good idea to clear a text field first, then send keys to it.

```
driver.find_element_by_name("username").send_keys("test")
driver.find_element_by_name("username").send_keys(" wisely") #=>'test wisely'
driver.find_element_by_name("username").clear()
driver.find_element_by_name("username").send_keys("agileway")
```

5.5 Enter text into a multi-line text area

Selenium treats text areas the same as text fields.

```
driver.find_element_by_id("comments").send_keys("Automated testing is\r\nFun\
!")
```

The "\r\n" represents a new line.

5.6 Assert value

```
driver.find_element_by_id("user").send_keys("testwisely")
assertEqual(driver.find_element_by_id("user").get_attribute("value"), "testw\
isely")
```

5.7 Focus on a control

Once we identify one control, we can set the focus on it. There is no *focus* function on *element* in Selenium, we can achieve 'focusing a control' by sending empty keystrokes to it.

```
driver.find_element_by_id("pass").send_keys("")
```

Or using JavaScript.

```
the_elem = driver.find_element_by_id("pass")
driver.execute_script("arguments[0].focus();", the_elem)
```

This workaround can be quite useful. When testing a long web page and some controls are not visible, trying to click them might throw "Element is not visible" error. In that case, setting the focus on the element might make it a visible.

5.8 Set a value to a read-only or disabled text field

'Read only' and 'disabled' text fields are not editable and are shown differently in the browser (typically grayed out).

```
Read only text field:
<input type="text" name="readonly_text" readonly="true"/> <br/>
Disabled text field:
<input type="text" name="disabled_text" disabled="true"/>
```

If a text box is set to be read-only, the following test step will not work.

```
driver.find_element_by_name("readonly_text").send_keys("new value")
```

Here is a workaround:

```
driver.execute_script("$('#readonly_text').val('bypass');")
assertEqual(driver.find_element_by_id("readonly_text").get_attribute("value"\
), "bypass")
driver.execute_script("$('#disabled_text').val('bypass');")
```

The below is a screenshot of a disabled and read-only text fields that were 'injected' with two values by the above test script.

Disabled text field: anyuse
Readonly text field: bypass

5.9 Set and assert the value of a hidden field

A hidden field is often used to store a default value.

```
<input type="hidden" name="currency" value="USD"/>
```

The below test script asserts the value of the above hidden field and changes its value using JavaScript.

```
the_hidden_elem = driver.find_element_by_name("currency")
assertEqual(the_hidden_elem.get_attribute("value"), "USD")
driver.execute_script("arguments[0].value = 'AUD';", the_hidden_elem)
assertEqual(driver.find_element_by_name("currency").get_attribute("value"), \
"AUD")
```

6. Radio button

◉ Male
◯ Female

HTML Source

```
<input type="radio" name="gender" value="male" id="radio_male" checked="true\
">Male<br>
<input type="radio" name="gender" value="female" id="radio_female">Female
```

6.1 Select a radio button

```
driver.find_element_by_xpath("//input[@name='gender' and @value='female']").\
click()
time.sleep(0.5)
driver.find_element_by_xpath("//input[@name='gender' and @value='male']").cl\
ick()
```

The radio buttons in the same radio group have the same name. To click one radio option, the value needs to be specified. Please note that the value is not the text shown next to the radio button, that is the label. To find out the value of a radio button, inspect the HTML source.

As always, if there are IDs, using by_id locator is easier.

```
driver.find_element_by_id("radio_female").click()
```

6.2 Clear radio option selection

It is OK to click a radio button that is currently selected, however, it would not have any effect.

```
driver.find_element_by_id("radio_female").click()
# already selected, no effect
driver.find_element_by_id("radio_female").click()
```

Once a radio button is selected, you cannot just clear the selection in Selenium. (Watir, another test framework, can clear radio selection). You need to select another radio button. The test script below will throw an error: "invalid element state: Element must be user-editable in order to clear it."

```
driver.find_element_by_xpath("//input[@name='gender' and @value='female']").\
click()
    try:
        driver.find_element_by_xpath("//input[@name='gender' and @value='fem\
ale']").clear()
    except:
        # Selenium does not allow
        print("Selenium does not allow clear currently selected radio button\
, just select another one")
        driver.find_element_by_xpath("//input[@name='gender' and @value='mal\
e']").click()
```

6.3 Assert a radio option is selected

The below script ensures the radio button is selected.

```
driver.find_element_by_xpath("//input[@name='gender' and @value='female']").\
click()
assertTrue(driver.find_element_by_xpath("//input[@name='gender' and @value='\
female']").is_selected())
```

6.4 Iterate radio buttons in a radio group

So far we have been focusing on identifying web controls by using one type of locator find_-element. Here I introduce another type of locator (I call them plural locators): find_elements.

```
assertEqual(len(driver.find_elements_by_name("gender")), 2)
for rb in driver.find_elements_by_name("gender"):
    if rb.get_attribute("value") == "female":
        rb.click()
```

Different from `find_element_by_` which returns one matched control, `find_elements_by_-`
return a list of them (also known as an array) back. This can be quite handy especially when
controls are hard to locate.

6.5 Click Nth radio button in a group

```
driver.find_elements_by_name("gender")[1].click()
assertTrue(driver.find_element_by_xpath("//input[@name='gender' and @value='\
female']").is_selected())
driver.find_elements_by_name("gender")[0].click()
assertTrue(driver.find_element_by_xpath("//input[@name='gender' and @value='\
male']").is_selected())
```

Once I was testing an online calendar, there were many time-slots, and the HTML
for each of these time-slots were exactly the same. I simply identified the time
slot by using the index (as above) on one of these 'plural' locators.

6.6 Click radio button by the following label

Some .NET controls generate poor quality HTML fragments like the one below:

```
<div id="q1" class="question">
  <div class="question-answer col-lg-5">
    <div class="yes-no">
      <input id="QuestionViewModels_1__SelectedAnswerId" name="QuestionViewM\
odels[1].SelectedAnswerId" type="radio" value="c225306e-8d8e-45b0-8261-22617\
d9796b5">
      <label for="QuestionViewModels_1__SelectedAnswerId">Yes</label>
    </div>
    <div class="yes-no">
      <input id="QuestionViewModels_1__SelectedAnswerId" name="QuestionViewM\
odels[1].SelectedAnswerId" type="radio" value="85ff8db7-1c58-47a2-a978-58120\
0fb7098">
      <label for="QuestionViewModels_1__SelectedAnswerId">No</label>
    </div>
  </div>
</div>
```

The id attribute of the above two radio buttons are the same, and the values are meaningless to human. The only thing can be used to identify a radio button is the text in label elements. The solution is to use XPath locator. You might have noticed that input (radio button) and label are siblings in the HTML DOM tree. We can use this relation to come up a XPath that identifies the label text, then the radio button.

```
elem = driver.find_element_by_xpath("//div[@id='q1']//label[contains(.,'Yes'\
)]/../input[@type='radio']")
elem.click()
```

6.7 Customized Radio buttons - iCheck

There are a number of plugins that customize radio buttons into a more stylish form, like the one below (using iCheck).

Gender: ✓ Male   ◯ Female

The iCheck JavaScript transforms the radio button HTML fragment

```
<input type="radio" name="sex" id="q2_1" value="male"> Male
```

to

```
<div class="iradio_square-red" style="position: relative;">
    <input type="radio" name="sex" id="q2_1" value="male" styl="....
    <ins class="iCheck-helper" style="...
</div>
```

Here are test scripts to drive iCheck radio buttons.

```
# Error: Element is not clickable
# driver.find_element_by_id("q2_1").click

driver.find_elements_by_class_name("iradio_square-red")[0].click()
driver.find_elements_by_class_name("iradio_square-red")[1].click()

# More precise with XPath
driver.find_element_by_xpath("//div[contains(@class, 'iradio_square-red')]/i\
nput[@type='radio' and @value='male']/..").click()
```

7. CheckBox

☐ I have a bike
☑ I have a car

HTML Source

```
<input type="checkbox" name="vehicle_bike" value="on" id="checkbox_bike">I h\
ave a bike<br>
<input type="checkbox" name="vehicle_car" id="checkbox_car">I have a car
```

7.1 Select by name

```
driver.find_element_by_name("vehicle_bike").click()
```

Clicking a checkbox, in fact, is a toggle, i.e, first click checks and the next one unchecks.

7.2 Uncheck a checkbox

```
the_checkbox = driver.find_element_by_name("vehicle_bike")
the_checkbox.click()
if the_checkbox.is_selected():
    the_checkbox.click()
```

7.3 Assert a checkbox is checked (or not)

```
the_checkbox = driver.find_element_by_name("vehicle_bike")
if not the_checkbox.is_selected():
    the_checkbox.click()
assertTrue(the_checkbox.is_selected())
the_checkbox.click()
assertFalse(the_checkbox.is_selected())
```

7.4 Customized Checkboxes - iCheck

There are a number of plugins that customize radio buttons into a more stylish form, like the one below (using iCheck).

The iCheck JavaScript transforms the checkbox HTML fragment

```
<input type="checkbox" name="sports[]" value="Soccer">  Soccer <br/>
```

to

```
<div class="icheckbox_square-red" style="position: relative;">
    <input type="checkbox" name="sports[]" value="Soccer" style="....
    <ins class="iCheck-helper" style="...
</div>
```

Here are test scripts to drive iCheck checkboxes.

```
driver.find_elements_by_class_name("icheckbox_square-red")[0].click()
time.sleep(0.5) # add some delays for JavaScript to execute
driver.find_elements_by_class_name("icheckbox_square-red")[1].click()
time.sleep(0.5)
# More precise with XPath
driver.find_element_by_xpath("//div[contains(@class, 'icheckbox_square-red')\
]/input[@type='checkbox' and @value='Soccer']/..").click()
```

8. Select List

A Select list is also known as a drop-down list or combobox.

Make: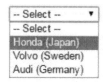

HTML Source

```
<select name="car_make" id="car_make_select">
  <option value="">-- Select --</option>
  <option value="honda">Honda (Japan)</option>
  <option value="volvo">Volvo (Sweden)</option>
  <option value="audi">Audi (Germany)</option>
</select>
```

8.1 Select an option by text

The label of a select list is what we can see in the browser.

```
from selenium import webdriver
from selenium.webdriver.support.ui import Select
Select(driver.find_element_by_name("car_make")).select_by_visible_text("Volv\
o (Sweden)")
```

8.2 Select an option by value

The value of a select list is what to be passed to the server.

```
Select(driver.find_element_by_name("car_make")).select_by_value("audi")
```

8.3 Select an option by iterating all options

Here I will show you a far more complex way to select an option in a select list, not for the sake of complexity, of course. A select list contains options, where each option itself is a valid control in Selenium.

```
my_select = driver.find_element_by_id("car_make_select")
for option in my_select.find_elements_by_tag_name("option"):
    if option.text == "Volvo (Sweden)":
        option.click()
        break
```

8.4 Select multiple options

A select list also supports multiple selections.

HTML Source

```
<select id="framework_select" name="test_framework" multiple="multiple">
  <option></option>
  <option value="rwebspec">RWebSpec</option>
  <option value="watir">Watir</option>
  <option value="selenium">Selenium</option>
</select>
```

```
select_box = Select(driver.find_element_by_name("test_framework"))
select_box.select_by_visible_text("Selenium")
select_box.select_by_visible_text("RWebSpec")
```

8.5 Clear one selection

```
select_box = Select(driver.find_element_by_name("test_framework"))
select_box.select_by_visible_text("Selenium")
select_box.select_by_value("rwebspec")
select_box.deselect_by_visible_text("RWebSpec") # by label
select_box.deselect_by_index(3) # :index
# now no options are selected
```

8.6 Clear selection

Clear selection works the same way for both single and multiple select lists.

```
select_box = Select(driver.find_element_by_name("test_framework"))
select_box.deselect_all()
```

8.7 Assert selected option

To verify a particular option is currently selected in a select list:

```
the_select = Select(driver.find_element_by_id("car_make_select"))
the_select.select_by_value("audi")
assertEqual(the_select.first_selected_option.text, "Audi (Germany)")
```

8.8 Assert the value of a select list

Another quick (and simple) way to check the current selected value of a select list:

```
the_select = Select(driver.find_element_by_name("car_make"))
the_select.select_by_visible_text("Volvo (Sweden)")
assertEqual(the_select.first_selected_option.get_attribute("value"), "volvo")
```

8.9 Assert multiple selections

A multiple select list can have multiple options being selected.

```
select_box = Select(driver.find_element_by_name("test_framework"))
select_box.select_by_visible_text("Selenium")
select_box.select_by_visible_text("RWebSpec")

selected = select_box.all_selected_options
assertEqual(2, len(selected))
assertEqual("RWebSpec", selected[0].text) # based on displaying order
assertEqual("Selenium", selected[1].text)
```

Please note, even though the test script selected 'Selenium' first, when it comes to assertion, the first selected option is 'RWebSpec', not 'Selenium'.

9. Navigation and Browser

Driving common web controls were covered from chapters 2 to 7. In this chapter, I will show how to manage browser windows and page navigation in them.

9.1 Go to a URL

```
driver.get("http://testwisely.com")
```

9.2 Visit pages within a site

`driver.get` takes a full URL. Most of time, testers test against a single site and specifying a full URL (such as `http://...`) is not necessary. We can create a reusable function to simplify its usage.

```
site_root_url = "http://test.testwisely.com" # test server

# ...

def visit(self, path):
    self.driver.get(self.site_root_url + path)

def test_go_to_page_within_the_site_using_function(self):
    self.visit("/demo")
    self.visit("/demo/survey")
    self.visit("/") # home page
```

Apart from being more readable, there is another benefit with this approach. If you want to run the same test against at a different server (the same application deployed on another machine), we only need to make one change: the value of $site_root_url.

```
site_root_url = "http://staging.testwisely.com" # another server
# ...
```

9.3 Perform actions from right mouse click context menu such as 'Back', 'Forward' or 'Refresh'

Operations with right click context menu are commonly page navigations, such as "Back to previous page". We can achieve the same by calling the test framework's navigation operations directly.

```
driver.back()
driver.refresh()
driver.forward()
```

9.4 Open browser in certain size

Many modern web sites use responsive web design, that is, page content layout changes depending on the browser window size. Yes, this increases testing effort, which means testers need to test web sites in different browser window sizes. Fortunately, Selenium has a convenient way to resize the browser window.

```
driver.set_window_size(1024, 768)
```

9.5 Maximize browser window

```
driver.maximize_window()
time.sleep(1)
driver.set_window_size(1024, 768)
```

9.6 Move browser window

We can move the browser window (started by the test script) to a certain position on screen, (0, 0) is the top left of the screen. The position of the browser's window won't affect the test results. This might be useful for utility applications, for example, a background video program can capture a certain area on screen.

```
driver.set_window_position(100, 200)
time.sleep(1)
driver.set_window_position(0, 0)
```

9.7 Minimize browser window

Surprisingly, there is no `minimize` window function in Selenium. The hack below achieves the same:

```
driver.set_window_position(-2000, 0)
driver.find_element_by_link_text("Hyperlink").click() # still can drive
time.sleep(2)
driver.set_window_position(0, 0)
```

While the browser's window is minimized, the test execution still can run.

9.8 Scroll focus to control

For certain controls are not viewable in a web page (due to JavaScript), WebDriver is unable to click on them by returning an error like *"Element is not clickable at point (1180, 43)"*. The solution is to scroll the browser view to the control.

```
elem = driver.find_element_by_name("submit_action_2")
elem_pos = elem.location["y"]
driver.execute_script("window.scroll(0, {})".format(elem_pos))
time.sleep(1)
elem.click()
```

9.9 Switch between browser windows or tabs

A "`target='_blank'`" hyperlink opens a page in another browser window or tab (depending on the browser setting). Selenium drives the browser within a scope of one browser window. However, we can use Selenium's `switch_to` function to change the target browser window.

```
driver.find_element_by_link_text("Hyperlink").click()
# target='_blank' link
driver.find_element_by_link_text("Open new window").click()
sdriver.switch_to.window(driver.window_handles[-1]) # switch to the last tab
assertIn("This is url link page", driver.find_element_by_tag_name("body").te\
xt)
driver.switch_to.window(driver.window_handles[0]) # back to first tab
assertTrue(driver.find_element_by_link_text("Open new window").is_displayed(\
))
```

9.10 Open new and close browser Tabs

To open a browser Tab, we can achieve by the JavaScript below.

```
driver.execute_script("window.open('http://facebook.com', '_blank')")
```

To close a browser Tab, make sure it is 'focused' (using `switch_to.window()`) and call `driver.close()`. Here is an example:

```
new_web_page_url = "http://clinicwise.net"
driver.execute_script("window.open('" + new_web_page_url + "', '_blank')")
tab_count = len(driver.window_handles)
# switch to the last tab
driver.switch_to.window(driver.window_handles[-1])
time.sleep(1)
driver.find_element_by_link_text("PRICING").click()
# now try to close first tab
driver.switch_to.window(driver.window_handles[0])
driver.find_element_by_link_text("Hyperlink").click()
driver.close()
assertEqual(tab_count - 1, len(driver.window_handles))
# re-focus
driver.switch_to.window(driver.window_handles[-1])
time.sleep(1)
driver.find_element_by_link_text("FEATURES").click()
```

Sending keystrokes such as Control + t to open a new browser tab does not work well. It might not work with latest version of Selenium WebDriver and your browser. Furthermore, the keystrokes on Mac are different: Command + t. Using JavaScript is easier.

9.11 Remember current web page URL, then come back to it later

We can store the page's URL into an instance variable (@url, for example).

```
url = driver.current_url
driver.find_element_by_link_text("Button").click()
# ...
time.sleep(1)
driver.get(url)
```

10. Assertion

Without assertions (or often known as checks), a test script is incomplete. Common assertions for testing web applications are:

- page title (equals)
- page text (contains or does not contain)
- page source (contains or does not contain)
- input element value (equals)
- display element text (equals)
- element state (selected, disabled, displayed)

10.1 Assert page title

```
assertEqual("Assertion Test Page", driver.title)
```

10.2 Assert Page Text

Example web page

```
Text assertion with a   (tab before), and
(new line before)!
```

HTML source

```
<PRE>Text assertion with a  (<b>tab</b> before), and
(new line before)!</PRE>
```

Test script

```
matching_str = "Text assertion with a  (tab before), and \n(new line before)\
 !"
assertIn(matching_str, driver.find_element_by_tag_name("body").text)
```

Please note the `find_element_by_tag_name("body").text` returns the text view of a web page after stripping off the HTML tags, but may not be exactly the same as we saw on the browser.

10.3 Assert Page Source

The page source is raw HTML returned from the server.

```
matching_html = "Text assertion with a  (<b>tab</b> before), and \n(new line\
 before)!"
assertIn(matching_html, driver.page_source)
```

10.4 Assert Label Text

HTML source

```
<label id="receipt_number">NB123454</label>
```

Label tags are commonly used in web pages to wrap some text. It can be quite useful to assert a specific text.

```
assertEqual("First Label", driver.find_element_by_id("label_1").text)
```

10.5 Assert Span text

HTML source

```
<span id="span_2">Second Span</span>
```

From testing perspectives, spans are the same as labels, just with a different tag name.

```
assertEqual("Second Span", driver.find_element_by_id("span_2").text)
```

10.6 Assert Div text or HTML

Example page

Wise Products
TestWise
BuildWise

HTML source

```
<div id="div_parent">
    Wise Products
    <div id="div_child_1">
      TestWise
    </div>
    <div id="div_child_2">
      BuildWise
    </div>
</div>
```

Test script

```
assertEqual("TestWise", driver.find_element_by_id("div_child_1").text)
assertEqual("Wise Products\nTestWise\nBuildWise", driver.find_element_by_id(\
"div_parent").text)
```

The below checks for the HTML fragment of an element.

```
the_element = driver.find_element_by_id("div_parent")
the_element_html = driver.execute_script("return arguments[0].outerHTML;", t\
he_element)
# print(the_element_html)
assertEqual(the_element_html, '<div id="div_parent">\n      Wise Products\n    \
  <div id="div_child_1">\n        TestWise\n      </div>\n      <div id="div_child\
_2">\n        BuildWise\n      </div>\n  </div>')
```

10.7 Assert Table text

HTML tables are commonly used for displaying grid data on web pages.

Example page

A	B
a	b

HTML source

```
<table id="aha_table" cellpadding="1" border="1" width="30%">
  <tr id="row_1">
    <td id="cell_1_1">A</td>
    <td id="cell_1_2">B</td>
  </tr>
  <tr id="row_2">
    <td id="cell_2_1">a</td>
    <td id="cell_2_2">b</td>
  </tr>
</table>
```

Test script

```
the_element = driver.find_element_by_id("alpha_table")
assertEqual(the_element.text, "A B\na b")
the_element_html = driver.execute_script("return arguments[0].outerHTML;", t\
he_element)
assertIn("<td id=\"cell_1_1\">A</td>", the_element_html)
```

10.8 Assert text in a table cell

If a table cell (td tag) has a unique ID, it is easy.

```
assertEqual("A", driver.find_element_by_id("cell_1_1").text)
```

An alternative approach is to identify a table cell using row and column indexes (both starting with 1).

```
assertEqual(driver.find_element_by_xpath("//table/tbody/tr[2]/td[2]").text, \
"b")
```

10.9 Assert text in a table row

```
assertEqual(driver.find_element_by_id("row_1").text, "A B")
```

10.10 Assert image present

```
assertTrue(driver.find_element_by_id("next_go").is_displayed())
```

10.11 Assert element location and width

```
image_elem = driver.find_element_by_id("next_go")
assertEqual(46, image_elem.size["width"])
assertTrue(image_elem.location["x"] > 100)
```

10.12 Assert element CSS style

```
elem = self.driver.find_element_by_id("highlighted")
assertEqual("15px", elem.value_of_css_property("font-size"))
assertEqual("rgba(206, 218, 227, 1)", elem.value_of_css_property("background\
-color"))
```

10.13 Assert JavaScript errors on a web page

JavaScripts errors can be inspected in browser's console. Here is how to detect JavaScript errors with Selenium WebDriver.

```
# a page with JavaScript errors
driver.get("http://testwisely.com/demo/customer-interview")
log_entries = driver.get_log("browser")
assertEqual(1, len(log_entries))
assertIn("net::ERR_CONNECTION_REFUSED", str(log_entries[0]))

# a page without errors
driver.get("http://testwisely.com/demo")
log_entries = driver.get_log("browser")
assertEqual(0, len(log_entries))
```

Please note this feature is browser dependent, it works on Chrome.

11. Frames

HTML Frames are treated as independent pages, which is not a good web design practice. As a result, few new sites use frames nowadays. However, there a quite a number of sites that uses iframes.

11.1 Testing Frames

Here is a layout of a fairly common frame setup: navigations on the top, menus on the left and the main content on the right.

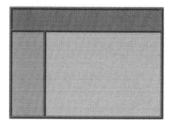

HTML Source

```
<frameset rows="100,*" frameborder="0" border="0" framespacing="0">
  <frame name="topNav" src="top_nav.html">
  <frameset cols="200,*" frameborder="0" border="0" framespacing="0">
    <frame name="menu" id="menu_frame" src="menu_1.html" marginheight="0" ma\
rginwidth="0" scrolling="auto" noresize>
    <frame name="content" src="content.html" marginheight="0" marginwidth="0\
" scrolling="auto" noresize>
  </frameset>
</frameset>
```

To test a frame with Selenium, we need to identify the frame first by ID or NAME, and then switch the focus on it. The test steps after will be executed in the context of selected frame. Use switch_to.default_content() to get back to the page (which contains frames).

```
driver.switch_to.frame("topNav")  # name
driver.find_element_by_link_text("Menu 2 in top frame").click()
# need to switch to default before another switch
driver.switch_to.default_content()
driver.switch_to.frame(driver.find_element_by_id("menu_frame"))
driver.find_element_by_link_text("Green Page").click()

driver.switch_to.default_content()
# for frame in frameset using name or ID
driver.switch_to.frame(driver.find_element_by_name("content"))
driver.find_element_by_link_text("Back to original page").click()
```

This script clicks a link in each of three frames: top, left menu and content.

11.2 Testing IFrame

An iframe (Inline Frame) is an HTML document embedded inside another HTML document on a web site.

Example page

Enter name: [   ]

Username: [   ]
Password: [   ]
[Login]

☐ I accept terms and conditions

HTML Source

```
<IFRAME frameborder='1' id="Frame1" src="login_iframe.html"
  Style="HEIGHT: 100px; WIDTH: 320px; MARGIN=0" SCROLLING="no" >
</IFRAME>
```

The test script below enters text in the main page, fills the sign in form in an iframe, and ticks the checkbox on the main page:

```
driver.get("file://" + self.site_url() + "/site/iframe.html")
driver.find_element_by_name("user").send_keys("agileway")
driver.switch_to.frame("Frame1")
driver.find_element_by_name("username").send_keys("tester")
driver.find_element_by_name("password").send_keys("TestWise")
driver.find_element_by_id("loginBtn").click()
assertIn("Signed in", driver.page_source)
driver.switch_to.default_content()
driver.find_element_by_id("accept_terms").click()
```

The web page after test execution looks as below:

Please note that the content of the iframe changed, but not the main page.

11.3 Test multiple iframes

A web page may contain multiple iframes.

```
driver.switch_to.frame(0)
driver.find_element_by_name("username").send_keys("agileway")
driver.switch_to.default_content()
driver.switch_to.frame(1)
driver.find_element_by_id("radio_male").click()
```

12. Testing AJAX

AJAX (an acronym for Asynchronous JavaScript and XML) is widely used in web sites nowadays (Gmail uses AJAX a lot). Let's look at an example first:

On clicking 'Transfer' button, an animated loading image showed up indicating 'transfer in progress'.

NetBank

To Account: Savings ▾

Enter Amount: 1200

Transfer

Receipt No: 6122
Receipt Date: **13/07/2016**

After the server processing the request, the loading image is gone and a receipt number is displayed.

From testing perspective, a test step (like clicking 'Transfer' button) is completed immediately. However the updates to parts of a web page may happen after unknown delay, which differs from traditional web requests.

There are 2 common ways to test AJAX operations: waiting enough time or checking the web page periodically for a maximum given time.

12.1 Wait within a time frame

After triggering an AJAX operation (clicking a link or button, for example), we can set a timer in our test script to wait for all the asynchronous updates to occur before executing next step.

```
driver.find_element_by_xpath("//input[@value='Transfer']").click()
time.sleep(10)
assertIn("Receipt No:", driver.find_element_by_tag_name("body").text)
```

`time.sleep(10)` means waiting for 10 seconds, after clicking 'Transfer' button. 10 seconds later, the test script will check for the 'Receipt No:" text on the page. If the text is present, the test passes; otherwise, the test fails. In other words, if the server finishes the processing and return the results correctly in 11 seconds, this test execution would be marked as 'failed'.

12.2 Explicit Waits until Time out

Apparently, the waiting for a specified time is not ideal. If the operation finishes earlier, the test execution would still be on halt. Instead of passively waiting, we can write test scripts to define a wait statement for certain condition to be satisfied until the wait reaches its timeout period. If Selenium can find the element before the defined timeout value, the code execution will continue to next line of code.

```
from selenium.webdriver.support.ui import WebDriverWait
from selenium.webdriver.support import expected_conditions as EC

#  ...

driver.find_element_by_xpath("//input[@value='Transfer']").click()
wait = WebDriverWait(driver, 10)
wait.until( EC.presence_of_element_located((By.ID, "receiptNo")) )
assertTrue(int( driver.find_element_by_id("receiptNo").text) > 0)
```

12.3 Implicit Waits until Time out

An implicit wait is to tell Selenium to poll finding a web element (or elements) for a certain amount of time if they are not immediately available. The default setting is 0. Once set, the implicit wait is set for the life of the WebDriver object instance, until its next set.

```
driver.find_element_by_xpath("//input[@value='Transfer']").click()
driver.implicitly_wait(10) # seconds
assertTrue(int( driver.find_element_by_id("receiptNo").text) > 0)
driver.implicitly_wait(0) # reset, don't wait any more
```

12.4 Create your own polling check function

The Explicit Waits and Implicit Waits in Selenium can be used to handle AJAX operation well. Here I want to show another rudimentary solution from different perspective.

```
driver.find_element_by_xpath("//input[@value='Transfer']").click() # AJAX
timeout = 10  # can change
start_time = datetime.datetime.now()
# print( (datetime.datetime.now() - start_time).seconds )
the_error_occurred = None
while ( (datetime.datetime.now() - start_time).seconds < timeout ):
    try:
        assertTrue( int(driver.find_element_by_id("receiptNo").text) > 0 )
        the_error_occurred = None
        break
    except:
        e = sys.exc_info()[0]
        the_error_occurred = e
        time.sleep(1) # polling interval
if (the_error_occurred):
    assertTrue( int(driver.find_element_by_id("receiptNo").text) > 0 )
```

12.5 Wait AJAX Call to complete using JQuery

If the target application uses JQuery for Ajax requests (most do), you may use a JavaScript call to check active Ajax requests: jQuery.active is a variable JQuery uses internally to track the number of simultaneous AJAX requests.

1. drive the control to initiate AJAX call
2. wait until the value of jQuery.active is zero
3. continue the next operation

The *waiting* is typically implemented in a reusable function.

```python
def test_wait_ajax_jquery(self):
  self.driver.get("http://travel.agileway.net")
  # ...
  self.driver.find_element_by_xpath("//input[@value='Pay now']").click()
  self.wait_for_ajax_complete(10)
  self.assertIn("Booking number", self.driver.page_source)

def wait_for_ajax_complete(self, max_seconds):
  count = 0
  while (count < max_seconds):
    count += 1
    is_ajax_complete = self.driver.execute_script("return window.jQuery != u\
ndefined && jQuery.active == 0");
    if is_ajax_complete:
      return
    else:
      time.sleep(1)
  raise Exception("Timed out after %i seconds" % max_seconds)
```

13. File Upload and Popup dialogs

In this chapter, I will show you how to handle file upload and popup dialogs. Most of pop up dialogs, such as 'Choose File to upload', are native windows rather than browser windows. This would be a challenge for testing as Selenium only drives browsers. If one pop up window is not handled properly, test execution will be on halt.

13.1 File upload

Example page

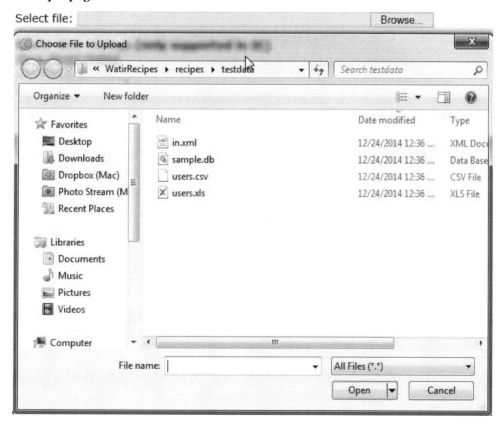

HTML Source

```
<input type="file" name="document[file]" id="files" size="60"/>
```

Test script

```
driver.find_element_by_name("document[file]").send_keys("C:\\testdata\\logo.\
png")
```

The first slash of \\ is for escaping the later one, the whole purpose is to pass the value "C:\testdata\logo.png" to the control.

Some might say, hard coding a file path is not a good practice. It's right, it is generally better to include your test data files within your test project, then use relative paths to refer to them, as the example below:

```
selected_file = os.path.join( os.path.dirname(os.path.realpath(__file__)), "\
testdata", "users.csv")
driver.find_element_by_name("document[file]").send_keys(selected_file)
```

13.2 JavaScript pop ups

JavaScript pop ups are created using javascript, commonly used for confirmation or alerting users.

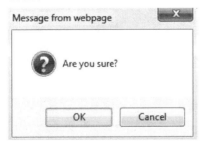

There are many discussions on handling JavaScript Pop ups in forums and Wikis. I tried several approaches. Here I list two stable ones:

Handle JavaScript pop ups using Alert API

```
driver.find_element_by_xpath("//input[contains(@value, 'Buy Now')]").click()
a = driver.switch_to.alert
print(a.text)
if a.text == 'Are you sure?':
    a.accept()
else:
    a.dismiss()
```

Handle JavaScript pop ups with JavaScript

```
driver.execute_script("window.confirm = function() { return true; }")
driver.execute_script("window.alert = function() { return true; }")
driver.execute_script("window.prompt = function() { return true; }")
driver.find_element_by_id("buy_now_btn").click()
```

Different from the previous approach, the pop up dialog is not even shown.

This recipe is courtesy of Alister Scott's WatirMelon blog[1]

13.3 Modal style dialogs

Flexible Javascript libraries, such as Bootstrap Modals[2], replace the default JavaScript alert dialogs used in modern web sites. Strictly speaking, a modal dialog like the one below is not a pop-up.

Comparing to the raw JS *alert*, writing automated tests against modal popups is easier.

---

[1]http://watirmelon.com/2010/10/31/dismissing-pesky-javascript-dialogs-with-watir/
[2]http://getbootstrap.com/javascript/#modals

```
driver.find_element_by_id("bootbox_popup").click()
time.sleep(0.5)
driver.find_element_by_xpath("//div[@class='modal-footer']/button[text()='OK\
']").click()
```

13.4 Bypass basic authentication by embedding username and password in URL

Authentication dialogs, like the one below, can be troublesome for automated testing.

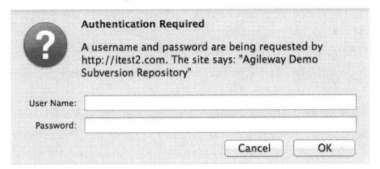

A very simple way to get pass Basic or NTLM authentication dialogs: prefix username and password in the URL.

```
driver.get("http://tony:password@itest2.com/svn-demo")
# got in, click a link
driver.find_element_by_link_text("tony/").click()
```

13.5 Internet Explorer modal dialog

Modal dialog, only supported in Internet Explorer, is a dialog (with 'Webpage dialog' suffix in title) that user has to deal with before interacting with the main web page. It is considered as a bad practice, and it is rarely found in modern web sites. However, some unfortunate testers might have to deal with modal dialogs.

Example page

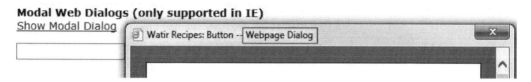

Modal Web Dialogs (only supported in IE)

HTML Source

```
<a href="javascript:void(0);" onclick="window.showModalDialog('button.html')\
">Show Modal Dialog</a>
```

Test script

```
river.find_element_by_link_text("Show Modal Dialog").click()
time.sleep(1)
driver.switch_to.window(driver.window_handles[-1]) # switch to the modal win
driver.find_element_by_name("user").send_keys("in_modal")
driver.switch_to.window(driver.window_handles[0]) # switch to the main win
driver.find_element_by_name("status").send_keys("done")
```

13.6 Popup Handler Approach

There are other types of pop ups too, such as Basic Authentication and Security warning dialogs. How to handle them? The fundamental difficulty behind pop up dialog handling is that some of these dialogs are native windows, not part of the browser, which means they are beyond the testing library's (i.e. Selenium) control.

Here I introduce a generic approach to handle all sorts of pop up dialogs. Set up a monitoring process (let's call it popup handler) waiting for notifications of possible new pop ups. Once the popup hander receives one, it will try to handle the pop up dialog with data received using windows automation technologies. It works like this:

```
# ...
NOTIFY_HANDLER_ABOUT_TO_TRIGGER_A_POPUP_OPERATION
PERFORM_OPERATION
# ...
```

BuildWise Agent[3] is a tool for executing automated tests on multiple machines in parallel. It has a free utility named 'Popup handler' just does that.

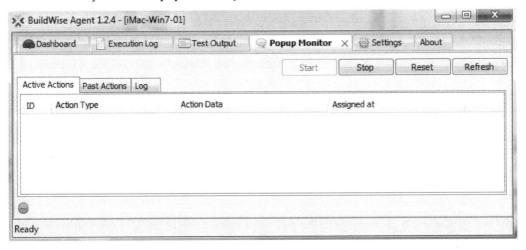

13.7 Handle JavaScript dialog with Popup Handler

```
# this will click 'OK' in popup window
handle_popup("javascript") {
  driver.find_element_by_path("//input[contains(@value, 'Buy Now')]").click()
}
```

The handle_popup is a function defined in *popup_handler_helper.py*, which is included in the same project.

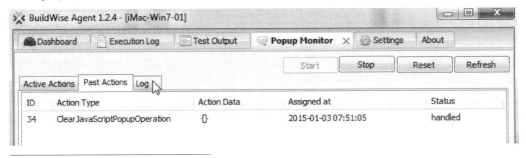

---

[3]http://testwisely.com/buildwise

13.8 Basic or Proxy Authentication Dialog

```
handle_popup("basic_auth",
    { :username => "tony", :password => "password",
        :win_title => "Connect to"}) {
  driver.get("http://itest2.com/svn-demo/")
}
driver.find_element_by_link_text("tony/").click
```

The same test steps can also be applied to proxy authentication dialogs.

14. Debugging Test Scripts

Debugging usually means analyzing and removing bugs in the code. In the context of automated functional testing, debugging is to find out why a test step did not execute as expected and fix it.

14.1 Print text for debugging

```
print("Now on page: " + driver.title)
app_no = driver.find_element_by_id("app_id").text
print("Application number is " + app_no)
```

Here is the output from executing the above test from command line:

```
Now on page: Assertion Test Page
Application number is 1234
```

When the test is executed in a Continuous Integration server, output is normally captured and shown. This can be quite helpful on debugging test execution.

14.2 Write page source or element HTML into a file

When the text you want to inspect is large (such as the page source), printing out the text to a console will not be helpful (too much text). A better approach is to write the output to a temporary file and inspect it later. It is often a better way to write to a temporary file, and use some other tool to inspect later.

```
file = open("c:\\temp\\login_page.html", "w", encoding='utf-8') # optional
file.write(driver.page_source); # whole page
file.close()
```

You can also just dump a specific part of web page:

```
the_element = driver.find_element_by_id("div_parent")
the_element_html = driver.execute_script("return arguments[0].outerHTML;", t\
he_element)
f = open("c:\\temp\\login_parent.xhtml", "w")
f.write(the_element_html)
f.close()
```

14.3 Take screenshot

Taking a screenshot of the current browser window when an error/failure happened is a good debugging technique. Selenium supports it in a very easy way.

```
driver.save_screenshot("C:\\temp\\screenshot.png")
# or
driver.get_screenshot_as_file("C:\\temp\\another_screenshot.png")
```

The above works. However, when it is run the second time, it will return error "The file already exists". A simple workaround is to write a file with timestamped file name, as below:

```
# save to timestamped file, e.g. screenshot-04071544.png
driver.save_screenshot("C:\\screenshot-#{Time.now.strftime('%m%d%H%M')}.png")
```

14.4 Leave browser open after test finishes

Once an error or failure occurred during test execution, a tester's immediate instinct is to check two things: which test statement is failed on and what current web page is like. The first one can be easily found in the testing tools (or command line output). We need the browser to stay open to see the web page. However, we don't want that when running a group of tests, as it will affect the execution of the following test cases.

Usually we put browser closing statements in tearDownClass() or tearDown() fixtures like the below:

```
@classmethod
def tearDownClass(cls):
    # print("Class teardown")
    cls.driver.quit()
```

Ideally, we would like to keep the browser open when after running an individual test case and close the browser when running multiple test script files, within the IDE. TestWise[1], an IDE for Selenium Ruby, has this feature. It maybe a possible extension you can add to your Python IDE. What I can tell you is that this feature is quite useful.

14.5 Debug test execution using Debugger

Pause, stop execution and run up to a certain statement are typical debugging features in programming IDEs.

Enable breakpoints

A breakpoint is a stoping or pausing place for debugging purposes. To set a breakpoint, mouse click the left margin next to the line you want to set the breakpoint in. After set, the statement line where the breakpoint is highlighted.

```
26      def test_wait_specified_time_for_ajax(self):
27          Select(self.driver.find_element_by_name("account")).select_by_visible_text
28          self.driver.find_element_by_id("rcptAmount").send_keys("250")
29          self.driver.find_element_by_xpath("//input[@value='Transfer']").click()
```

You may set more than one breakpoints.

Execute one test case in debugging mode

To start debugging one test case, right mouse click within the lines of the selected test case and select 'Debug Tests'.

---

[1]http://testwisely.com/testwise

Test execution starts (will be littler slower in debugging mode),

```
26    ⊟    def test_wait_specified_time_for_ajax(self):
27              Select(self.driver.find_element_by_name("account")).select_by_visible_text
28    ●         self.driver.find_element_by_id("rcptAmount").send_keys("250")
29              self.driver.find_element_by_xpath("//input[@value='Transfer']").click()
30              time.sleep(10)
```

Once the test execution is on halt, you can do inspection against the web page.

Step over test execution

To continue test execution, click the 'Step over' button on the tool bar.

```
27           Select(self.driver.find_element_by_name("account")).select_by_visible_text(
28    ●      self.driver.find_element_by_id("rcptAmount").send_keys("250")
29           self.driver.find_element_by_xpath("//input[@value='Transfer']").click()
```
ase.test Step Over (F8) time_for_ajax

This will execute the just one test statement line, after that, the execution remains in pausing mode again.

```
28    ●         self.driver.find_element_by_id("rcptAmount").send_keys("250")
29              self.driver.find_element_by_xpath("//input[@value='Transfer']").click()
```

15. Test Data

Gathering test data is an important but often neglected activity. Thanks to the power and flexibility of Python, testers now have a new ability to prepare test data.

15.1 Get date dynamically

```
import datetime
# assume today is 2015-04-14
print(datetime.date.today())   # => 2015-04-14
print(datetime.datetime.now()) # =>  2015-04-14 18:49:48.154616
```

Based on the above, we can create easy to read date related functions (see the helper method in the sample project), like the one below

```
# default to UK/AUS date format
def today(self, format = "%Y-%m-%d"):
  return datetime.date.today().strftime(format)
```

Then you can use the following in your test scripts.

```
today()            #=> 2015-04-14
today("%m/%d/%Y")  #=> 04/14/2015
```

Based on this, we can write more date helper methods.

```
yesterday()        # 2015-04-13
tomorrow()         # 2015-04-15
days_from_now(3)   # 2015-04-17
days_before(3)     # 2015-04-11
```

Example use

```
assertEqual(driver.find_element_by_id("date").text, today())
```

15.2 Get a random boolean value

A boolean value means either *true* or *false*. Getting a random true or false might not sound that interesting. That was what I thought when I first learned it. Later, I realized that it is actually very powerful, because I can fill the computer program (test script as well) with nondeterministic data.

```
import random

random.choice([True, False]   # True or False
```

For example, in a user sign up form, we could write two cases: one for male and one for female. With random boolean, I could achieve the same with just one test case. If the test case get run many times, it will cover both scenarios.

```
random_value = "male" if random.choice([True, False]) else "female"
elem = driver.find_element_by_xpath("//input[@type='radio' and @name='gender\
' and @value='" + random_value + "']")
elem.click()
```

15.3 Generate a number within a range

```
random.randint(10, 99) a random number 10 up to 99 (inclusive), different ea\
ch run
```

The test statement below will enter a number between 16 to 99. If the test gets run hundreds of times, not a problem at all for an automated test, it will cover driver's input for all permitted ages.

```
driver.find_element_by_id("drivers_age").send_keys(random.randint(16, 99))
```

15.4 Get a random character

```
import random
import string

random.choice(string.ascii_letters)    # eg. 't' or 'A'
random.choice(string.ascii_lowercase)
random.choice(string.ascii_uppercase)
```

15.5 Get a random string at fixed length

```
# generate 10 characters lower case string
''.join(random.choice(string.ascii_lowercase) for _ in range(10))

# generate a password with Mixed case + digits exactly 8 characters
random.choice(string.ascii_uppercase) + random.choice(string.digits) + ''.jo\
in(random.choice(string.ascii_lowercase) for _ in range(6))
# 'D1cmuqry'
```

The above statement is quite complex. By creating some utility functions (you can find in source project), we can get quite readable test scripts as below:

```
debug random_str(7) #  example: "dolorem"
debug words(5) #  example: "sit doloremque consequatur accusantium aut"
debug sentences(3)
debug paragraphs(2)
```

15.6 Get a random string in a collection

```
random.sample(["Yes", "No", "Maybe"], 1)  # one of these strings
```

I frequently use this in my test scripts.

15.7 Generate random person names, emails, addresses with Faker

Faker[1] is a Python library that generates fake data.

---

[1]https://github.com/joke2k/faker

```
from faker import Faker
fake = Faker()

fake.name()     # => "Jeromy Erdman"
fake.address()  # => "514 Daugherty Plain\nNikolausburgh, DC 30871"
fake.email()    # tyrek.welch@konopelski.biz
```

You can find more examples at Faker[2] website. By default, addresses and phone numbers are US format, however, you can switch to another locale.

15.8 Generate a test file at fixed sizes

When testing file uploads, testers often try test files in different sizes. The following Python statement generates a test file in precise size on the fly.

```
file_name = os.path.join(os.path.dirname(os.path.realpath(__file__)), "tmp",\
  "2MB.txt")
with open(file_name, 'w') as f:
  f.write(1024 * 1024 * 2 * '0')
```

15.9 Retrieve data from Database

The ultimate way to obtain accurate test data is to retrieve from the database. For many projects, this might not be possible. For ones do, this provides the ultimate flexibility in terms of getting test data.

The test script example below is to enter the oldest (by age) user's login into the text field on a web page. To get this oldest user in the system, I use SQL to query the database directly (SQlite3 in this example, it will be different for yours, but the concept is the same).

---

[2]https://github.com/joke2k/faker

```python
import sqlite3

# ...

db = sqlite3.connect( os.path.join( os.path.dirname(os.path.realpath(__file_\
_)), "testdata", "sample.db"))
# Users table: with login, name, age
cursor = db.cursor()
oldest_user_login = None
cursor.execute( "select * from users order by age desc" )
first_row = cursor.fetchone()
# print(first_row)
oldest_user_login = first_row[0]

assertEqual("mark", oldest_user_login)
driver.get("file:///C:/work/books/SeleniumRecipes-Python/site/text_field.htm\
l")
driver.find_element_by_id("user").send_keys(oldest_user_login)
```

16. Browser Profile and Capabilities

Selenium can start browser instances with various profile preferences which can be quite useful. Obviously, some preference settings are browser specific, so you might take some time to explore. In this chapter, I will cover some common usage.

16.1 Get browser type and version

Detecting browser type and version is useful to write custom test scripts for different browsers.

```
driver = webdriver.Chrome()
print(driver.capabilities["browserName"]) # => chrome
print(driver.capabilities["platform"])    # => Windows NT
print(driver.capabilities["version"])     # => 42.0.2311.90
driver.quit()


driver = webdriver.Firefox()
assertEqual("firefox", driver.capabilities["browserName"])
if os.name == "Darwin":
    assertEqual("darwin", driver.capabilities["platform"]) # Mac
elif os.name == "nt":
    # old versions return :winnt
    assertEqual(driver.capabilities["platform"], "WINDOWS")
print(driver.capabilities["version"]) # => 37.0.2
driver.quit()



driver = Selenium::WebDriver.for(:ie)
print(driver.capabilities["browserName"]) # "internet explorer"
```

16.2 Set HTTP Proxy for Browser

Here is an example to set HTTP proxy server for Firefox browser.

```
fp = webdriver.FirefoxProfile()
fp.set_preference('network.proxy.type',  1)
# http://kb.mozillazine.org/Network.proxy.type
fp.set_preference('network.proxy.http', "myproxy.com")
fp.set_preference('network.proxy.http_port',  3128)
driver = webdriver.Firefox(firefox_profile=fp)
driver.get("http://testwisely.com/demo")
driver.quit()
```

16.3 Verify file download in Chrome

To efficiently verify a file is downloaded, we would like

- save the file to a specific folder
- avoid "Open with or Save File" dialog


```
chromeOptions = webdriver.ChromeOptions()
prefs = {"download.default_directory" : "C:\TEMP" if os.name == "nt" else "/\
Users/zhimin/tmp" }
chromeOptions.add_experimental_option("prefs", prefs)
driver = webdriver.Chrome(chrome_options=chromeOptions)
driver.get("http://zhimin.com/books/pwta")
driver.find_element_by_link_text("Download").click()
time.sleep(15) # wait download to complete
if os.name == "nt":
  assertTrue( os.path.isfile("c:/TEMP/practical-web-test-automation-sample.p\
df") )
else:
  assertTrue( os.path.isfile("/Users/zhimin/tmp/practical-web-test-automatio\
n-sample.pdf") )
driver.quit()
```

This is the new way (from v2.37) to pass preferences to Chrome.

More Chrome preferences: http://src.chromium.org/svn/trunk/src/chrome/common/pref_-names.cc[1]

---

[1]http://src.chromium.org/svn/trunk/src/chrome/common/pref_names.cc

16.4 Test downloading PDF in Firefox

```
fp = webdriver.FirefoxProfile()
fp.set_preference("browser.download.folderList", 2)
fp.set_preference("browser.download.dir", "C:\TEMP" if os.name == "nt" else \
"/Users/zhimin/tmp")
fp.set_preference("browser.helperApps.neverAsk.saveToDisk", 'application/pdf\
')
fp.set_preference('browser.download.manager.showWhenStarting', False)
# disable Firefox's built-in PDF viewer
fp.set_preference("pdfjs.disabled", True)


driver = webdriver.Firefox(fp)
driver.get("http://zhimin.com/books/selenium-recipes")
driver.find_element_by_link_text("Download").click()
time.sleep(10 )# wait download to complete
if os.name == "nt":
  assertTrue( os.path.isfile("c:/TEMP/selenium-recipes-in-ruby-sample.pdf") )
else:
  assertTrue( os.path.isfile("/Users/zhimin/tmp/selenium-recipes-in-ruby-sam\
ple.pdf") )
driver.quit()
```

16.5 Bypass basic authentication with Firefox AutoAuth plugin

There is another complex but quite useful approach to bypass basic authentication: use a browser extension. Take Firefox for example, "Auto Login"[2] submits HTTP authentication dialogs remembered passwords.

By default, Selenium starts Firefox with an empty profile, which means no remembered passwords and extensions. We can instruct Selenium to start Firefox with an existing profile.

- Start Firefox with a dedicated profile. Run the command below (from command line) Windows:

---

[2]https://addons.mozilla.org/en-US/firefox/addon/autoauth/

```
"C:\Program Files (x86)\Mozilla Firefox\firefox.exe" -p
```

Mac:

```
/Applications/Firefox.app/Contents/MacOS/firefox-bin  -p
```

- Create a profile (I name it 'testing') and start Firefox with this profile

- Install autoauth plugin. A simple way: drag the file *autoauth-2.1-fx+fn.xpi* (included with the test project) to Firefox window.

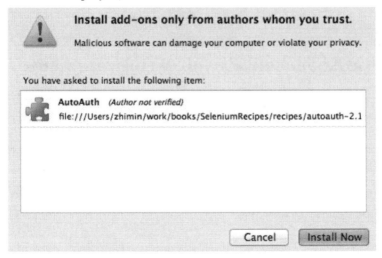

- Visit the web site requires authentication. Manually type the user name and password. Click 'Remember Password'.

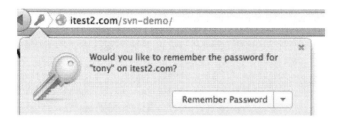

Now the preparation work is done (and only need to be done once).

```
# Prerequisite: the password is already remembered in 'testing' profile.
fp = webdriver.FirefoxProfile( os.environ['APPDATA'] + "\\Mozilla\\Firefox\\\
Profiles\\i0rdlto9.testing")
fp.add_extension(os.path.join( os.path.dirname(os.path.realpath(__file__)), \
'autoauth-2.1-fx+fn.xpi'))
# Auto Login inform saved  https://addons.mozilla.org/en-US/firefox/addon/au\
toauth/
driver = webdriver.Firefox(fp)
driver.get("http://itest2.com/svn-demo/")
driver.find_element_by_link_text("tony/").click()
```

The hardcoded profile path `tcfyedtq.testing` is not ideal, as the test script will fail when running on another machine. The code below will get around that.

```
def get_firefox_profile_folder_by_name(self, profile_name):
    FF_PROFILE_PATH = os.path.join(os.environ['APPDATA'], 'Mozilla', 'Firefo\
x', 'Profiles')
    # profile dir will digest.name such as i0rdlto9.testing
    try:
        profiles = os.listdir(FF_PROFILE_PATH)
    except WindowsError:
        print("Could not find profiles directory.")
        raise

    loc = None
    try:
        for dir in profiles:
            if dir.endswith(profile_name):
```

```
            loc = dir
            break
except StopIteration:
    print("Firefox profile not found.")
    raise


profile_path = os.path.join(FF_PROFILE_PATH, loc)
return profile_path


# ...
# in your test case
ff_profile_dir = self.get_firefox_profile_folder_by_name("testing")
fp = webdriver.FirefoxProfile(ff_profile_dir)
```

16.6 Manage Cookies

```
driver.get("http://travel.agileway.net")
cookie = { 'name' : 'foo', 'value' : 'bar'}
driver.add_cookie(cookie)
cookies_list = driver.get_cookies()
print(cookies_list.__class__) # <class 'list'>
retrieved_cookie = driver.get_cookie("foo")
self.assertEqual("bar", retrieved_cookie["value"])
```

16.7 Headless browser testing with PhantomJS

A headless browser is a web browser without a graphical user interface. The main benefit of headless browser testing is performance. PhantomJS[3] is a headless browser that built on top of WebKit, the engine behind both Safari and Chrome. First of all, you need download phantomjs.exe and add it to PATH.

---

[3]http://phantomjs.org/

```
driver = webdriver.PhantomJS()
driver.get("http://travel.agileway.net")
driver.set_window_size(1024, 650)
assertEqual("Agile Travel", driver.title)
driver.quit
```

If your target application is relatively stable and not using JavaScript heavily, and you want gain test faster execution time, PhantomJS is a viable option.

Be aware of headless browser simulation in test automation

Frankly, I am not big fan of headless testing with browser simulation for the reasons below:

- It is NOT a real browser.
- I need inspect the web page when a test failed, I cannot do that with PhantomJS. In test automation, as we know, we perform this all the time.
- To achieve faster execution time, I prefer distributing tests to multiple build agents to rum them in parallel as a part of Continuous Testing process. That way, I get not only much faster execution time (throwing in more machines), also get useful features such as quick feedback, rerunning failed tests on another build agent, dynamic execution ordering by priority, etc. All in real browsers.

Update [April 13, 2017]: PhantomJS' maintainer stepped down[a], the future of PhantomJS is in doubt.

---

[a]https://groups.google.com/forum/m/#!topic/phantomjs/9aI5d-LDuNE

16.8 Headless Chrome

Chrome 59 (released on June 5, 2017) introduces headless mode, which can be used with Selenium WebDriver. Here is how:

```
chromeOptions = webdriver.ChromeOptions()
chromeOptions.add_argument("headless")
# for some chrome builds, may need switch "--disable-gpu"to avoid errors
driver = webdriver.Chrome(chrome_options=chromeOptions)
driver.get("http://travel.agileway.net")
self.assertEqual("Agile Travel", driver.title)
driver.quit()
```

Please note that, at the time of writing, Headless mode is available on Mac and Linux in Chrome 59, but Windows support[4] will be available soon.

16.9 Test responsive websites

Modern websites embrace responsive design to fit in different screen resolutions on various devices, such as iPad and smartphones. Bootstrap is a very popular responsive framework. How to verify your web site's responsiveness is a big question, it depends what you want to test. A quick answer is to use WebDriver's `driver.set_window_size` to set your browser to a target resolution, and then execute tests.

The example below verify a text box's width changes when switching from a desktop computer to a iPad, basically, whether responsive is enabled or not..

```
driver.set_window_size(1200, 800)  # Desktop
driver.get("http://agileway.net")
width_desktop = driver.find_element_by_name("email").size["width"]
driver.set_window_size(768, 1024)  # iPad
width_ipad = driver.find_element_by_name("email").size["width"]
assertTrue(width_desktop < width_ipad)  # 358 vs 1050
```

16.10 Set page load timeout

For tests checking maximum page response time specifically, we can set the timeout in the script like below:

---

[4]https://bugs.chromium.org/p/chromium/issues/detail?id=686608

```
driver = webdriver.Chrome()
driver.set_page_load_timeout(1)  # shall time out
driver.get("http://testwisely.com/demo")
```

If the response time exceeds 1 second, very likely so, you will see the test failed with the below error:

```
selenium.common.exceptions.TimeoutException: Message: timeout: cannot determ\
ine loading status
from timeout: Timed out receiving message from renderer:
```

17. Advanced User Interactions

The ActionChains in Selenium WebDriver provides a way to set up and perform complex user interactions. Specifically, grouping a series of keyboard and mouse operations and sending to the browser.

Mouse interactions

- click
- click_and_hold
- context_click
- double_click
- drag_and_drop
- drag_and_drop_by_offset
- move_by_offset
- move_to_element
- move_to_element_with_offset
- release

Keyboard interactions

- key_down
- key_up
- send_keys
- send_keys_to_element

The usage

ActionChains(driver). + one or more above operations + .perform()

Check out the ActionChains API[1] for more.

17.1 Double click a control

---

[1]http://selenium-python.readthedocs.io/api.html#module-selenium.webdriver.common.action_chains

```
elem = driver.find_element_by_id("pass")
ActionChains(driver).double_click(elem).perform()
```

17.2 Move mouse to a control - Mouse Over

```
elem = driver.find_element_by_id("email")
ActionChains(driver).move_to_element(elem).perform()
```

17.3 Click and hold - select multiple items

The test scripts below clicks and hold to select three controls in a grid.

```
driver.get("http://jqueryui.com/selectable")
driver.find_element_by_link_text("Display as grid").click()
time.sleep(0.5)
driver.switch_to.frame(0)
list_items = driver.find_elements_by_xpath("//ol[@id='selectable']/li")
ActionChains(driver).click_and_hold(list_items[1])\
    .click_and_hold(list_items[3])\
    .click()\
    .perform()
driver.switch_to.default_content()
```

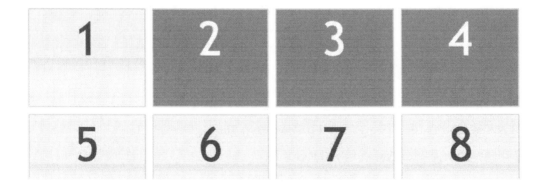

17.4 Context Click - right click a control

```
driver.get("file://"  + self.site_url() + "/site/text_field.html")
time.sleep(0.5)
elem = driver.find_element_by_id("pass")
# browser specific, paste text
if (driver.capabilities["browserName"] == "firefox"):
    ActionChains(driver).send_keys(Keys.DOWN)\
        .send_keys(Keys.DOWN)\
        .send_keys(Keys.DOWN)\
        .send_keys(Keys.DOWN)\
        .send_keys(Keys.RETURN)\
        .perform()
```

17.5 Drag and drop

Drag-n-drop is increasingly more common in new web sites. Testing this feature can be largely achieved in Selenium, I used the word 'largely' means achieving the same outcome, but not the 'mouse dragging' part. For this example page,

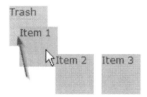

the test script below will *drop* 'Item 1' to 'Trash'.

```
drag_from = driver.find_element_by_id("item_1")
target = driver.find_element_by_id("trash")
ActionChains(driver).drag_and_drop(drag_from, target).perform()
```

The below is a screenshot after the test execution.

17.6 Drag slider

Slider (a part of JQuery UI library) provide users an very intuitive way to adjust values (typically in settings).

Slider

The test below simulates 'dragging the slider to the right'.

```
self.assertEqual(driver.find_element_by_id("pass_rate").text, "15%")
elem = driver.find_element_by_id("pass-rate-slider")
ActionChains(driver).drag_and_drop_by_offset(elem, 2, 0).perform()
# unable to set specific value
self.assertNotEqual(driver.find_element_by_id("pass_rate").text, "15%")
```

More information about `drag_and_drop_by_offset` can be found at Selenium WebDriver ActionChains API[2].

The below is a screenshot after the test execution.

Slider

Please note that the percentage figure after executing the test above are always 50% (I saw 49% now and then).

17.7 Send key sequences - Select All and Delete

---

[2]http://selenium-python.readthedocs.io/api.html#module-selenium.webdriver.common.action_chains

```
driver.get("file://"  + self.site_url() + "/site/text_field.html")
driver.find_element_by_id("comments").send_keys("Multiple Line\r\n Text")
elem = driver.find_element_by_id("comments")
ActionChains(driver).click(elem)\
    .key_down(Keys.CONTROL)\
    .send_keys("a")\
    .key_up(Keys.CONTROL)\
    .perform()
# this different from click element, the key is send to browser directly
ActionChains(driver).send_keys(Keys.BACKSPACE).perform()
```

Please note that the last test statement is different from `elem.send_keys`. The keystrokes triggered by `ActionChains.send_keys` is sent to the active browser window, not a specific element.

17.8 Click a specific part of an image

The image below contains special marked areas (appears on mouse over) linked to different URLs.

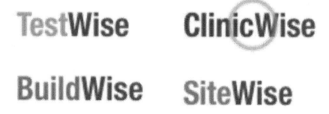

Here is the HTML:

```
<img src='images/agileway_software.png'id="agileway_software" usemap="#agile\
way_software_map">
<map name="agileway_software_map" id="agileway_software_map">
    <area shape="rect" coords="10,60,120,88" href="https://testwisely.com/bu\
ildwise" alt="buildwise"/>
    <area shape="circle" coords="200,25,18" href="https://clinicwise.net" al\
t="clinicwise">
</map>
```

We can use `move_to_element_with_offset(elem, xoffset, yoffset)` to click specific co-ordinates.

```
driver.get("file://"  + self.site_url() + "/../site/image-map.html")
elem = driver.find_element_by_id("agileway_software")
ActionChains(self.driver).move_to_element_with_offset(elem, 190, 30).click()\
.perform()
assertEqual("ClinicWise - Cloud based Health Clinic Management System", self\
.driver.title)
driver.get("file://"  + self.site_url() + "/../site/image-map.html")
elem = driver.find_element_by_id("agileway_software")
ActionChains(self.driver).move_to_element_with_offset(elem, 30, 75).click().\
perform()
assertEqual("BuildWise - TestWisely", self.driver.title)
```

18. HTML 5 and Dynamic Web Sites

Web technologies are evolving. HTML5 includes many new features for more dynamic web applications and interfaces. Furthermore, wide use of JavaScript (thanks to popular JavaScript libraries such as JQuery), web sites nowadays are much more dynamic. In this chapter, I will show some Selenium examples to test HTML5 elements and interactive operations.

Please note that some tests only work on certain browsers (Chrome is your best bet), as some HTML5 features are not fully supported in some browsers yet.

18.1 HTML5 Email type field

Let's start with a simple one. An email type field is used for input fields that should contain an e-mail address. From the testing point of view, we treat it exactly the same as a normal text field.

Email field

jam

HTML Source

```
<input id="email" name="email" type="email" style="height:30px; width: 280px\
;">
```

```
driver.find_element_by_id("email").send_keys("test@wisely.com")
```

18.2 HTML5 Time Field

The HTML5 time field is much more complex, as you can see from the screenshot below.

Time

HTML Source

```
<input id="start_time_1" name="start_time" type="time" style="height:30px; w\
idth: 120px;">
```

The test scripts below do the following:

1. make sure the focus is not on this time field control
2. click and focus the time field
3. clear existing time
4. enter a new time

```
import time
from selenium.webdriver.common.keys import Keys

# focus on another ...
driver.find_element_by_id( "home_link").send_keys("")
time.sleep(0.5)

# now back to change it
driver.find_element_by_id( "start_time_1").click
driver.find_element_by_id( "start_time_1").send_keys([Keys.DELETE, Keys.LEFT\
, Keys.DELETE, Keys.LEFT, Keys.DELETE])

driver.find_element_by_id("start_time_1").send_keys("08")
time.sleep(0.3)
driver.find_element_by_id("start_time_1").send_keys("27")
time.sleep(0.3)
driver.find_element_by_id("start_time_1").send_keys("AM")
```

18.3 Invoke 'onclick' JavaScript event

In the example below, when user clicks on the text field control, the tip text (*'Max 20 characters'*) is shown.

Example page

Max 20 characters

HTML Source

```
<input type="text" name="person_name" onclick="$('#tip').show();"  onchange=\
"change_person_name(this.value);"/>
<span id="tip" style="display:none; margin-left: 20px; color:gray;">Max 20 c\
haracters</span>
```

When we use normal send_keys() in Selenium, it enters the text OK, but the tip text is not displayed.

```
driver.find_element_by_name("person_name").send_keys("Wise Tester")
```

We can simply call 'click' to achieve it.

```
driver.find_element_by_name("person_name").clear()
driver.find_element_by_name("person_name").send_keys("Wise Tester")
driver.find_element_by_name("person_name").click()
assertEqual(driver.find_element_by_id("tip").text, "Max 20 characters")
```

18.4 Invoke JavaScript events such as 'onchange'

A generic way to invoke 'OnXXXX' events is to execute JavaScript, the below is an example to invoke 'OnChange' event on a text box.

```
driver.find_element_by_name("person_name").clear()
driver.find_element_by_name("person_name").send_keys("Test Wise")
# another way
# driver.execute_script("return document.getElementById('person_name_textbox\
').fireEvent('OnChange')");
driver.execute_script("$('#person_name_textbox').trigger('change')");
assertEqual(driver.find_element_by_id("person_name_label").text, "Test Wise")
```

18.5 Scroll to the bottom of a page

Calling JavaScript API.

```
driver.execute_script("window.scrollTo(0, document.body.scrollHeight);")
```

Or send the keyboard command: 'Ctrl+End'.

```
driver.find_element_by_tag_name("body").send_keys([Keys.CONTROL, Keys.END])
# or
ActionChains(driver).key_down(Keys.CONTROL).send_keys(Keys.END).key_up(Keys.\
CONTROL).perform()
```

18.6 Select2 - Single Select

Select2 is a popular JQuery plug-in that makes long select lists more user-friendly, it turns the standard HTML select list box into this:

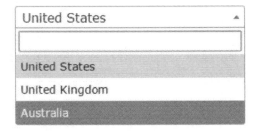

HTML Source

```
<select id="country_single" data-placeholder="Choose a Country..." class="se\
lect2">
   <option value=""></option>
   <option value="United States">United States</option>
   <option value="United Kingdom">United Kingdom</option>
   <option value="Australia">Australia</option>
</select>
```

The HTML source seems not much different from the standard select list excepting adding the class select2. By using the class as the identification, the JavaScript included on the page generates the following HTML fragment (beneath the select element).

Generated HTML Source

```
<select id="country_single" .... />
<span class="select2-container select2-container--default select2-container-\
-open"><span class="select2-dropdown select2-dropdown--below"><span class="s\
elect2-search select2-search--dropdown">
    <input autocomplete="off" class="select2-search__field" type="search">
 </span><span class="select2-results"></span></span></span>
<ul aria-expanded="true" aria-hidden="false" class="select2-results__options\
" id="select2-country_single-results" role="tree">
  <li aria-selected="false" class="select2-results__option select2-results__\
option--highlighted" id="select2-country_single-result-pvve-United States">
    <span class="select2-results">United States</span></li>
  <li aria-selected="false" class="select2-results__option" id="select2-coun\
try_single-result-orle-United Kingdom">
    <span class="select2-results">United Kingdom</span></li>
  <li aria-selected="false" class="select2-results__option" id="select2-coun\
try_single-result-kbxr-Australia">
    <span class="select2-results">Australia</span></li>
</ul>
```

Please note that this dynamically generated HTML fragment is not viewable by 'View Page Source', you need to enable the inspection tool (usually right mouse click the page, then choose 'Inspect Element') to see it.

Before we test it, we need to understand how we use it.

- Click the 'Choose a Country'
- Select an option

There is no difference from the standard select list. That's correct, we need to understand how Select2 emulates the standard select list first. In Select2, clicking the 'Choose a Country' (to show the options) is actually clicking the span next to the original <select> with id "country_single"; selecting an option is clicking a list item (tag: li) under ul with id 'select2-country_single-results'' (where 'country_single' is the ID of original Select). With these knowledge, plus XPath in Selenium, we can drive a Select2 standard select box with the test scripts below:

```
driver.get("file:" + self.site_url() + "/select2.html")
time.sleep(1) # wait enough time to load JS

driver.find_element_by_xpath("//select[@id='country_single']/../span").click\
()
available_items = driver.find_elements_by_xpath("//ul[@id='select2-country_s\
ingle-results']/li")
for x in available_items:
    if x.text == "Australia":
        x.click()
        break
```

A neat feature of Select2 is allowing user to search the option list, to do that in Selenium:

```
driver.find_element_by_xpath("//select[@id='country_single']/../span//span[@\
class='select2-selection__arrow']").click()
time.sleep(0.5)
search_text_field = driver.find_element_by_xpath("//span/input[@class = 'sel\
ect2-search__field']")
search_text_field.send_keys("United King")
time.sleep(0.5) # let filtering finishing
# select first highlighted option
search_text_field.send_keys(Keys.ENTER)
```

18.7 Select2 - Multiple Select

Select2[1] also enhances the multiple selection (a lot).

HTML Source

---

[1]https://github.com/select2/select2

```
<select id="country_multiple"  data-placeholder="Choose Countries..." class=\
"select2" multiple style="width:420px;">
  <option value=""></option>
  <option value="United States">United States</option>
  <option value="United Kingdom">United Kingdom</option>
  <option value="Australia">Australia</option>
</select>
```

Again, the only difference from the standard multiple select list is the class 'select2'. Astute readers will find the generated HTML fragment is different from the standard (single) select, that's because of the usage. The concept of working out driving the control is the same, I will leave the homework to you, just show the test scripts.

```
# click the box then select one option
select2_multi_container_xpath = "//select[@id='country_multiple']/../span[co\
ntains(@class, 'select2-container')]"
driver.find_element_by_xpath(select2_multi_container_xpath).click()
available_items = driver.find_elements_by_xpath("//ul[@id='select2-country_m\
ultiple-results']/li")
for x in available_items:
    if x.text == "Australia":
        x.click()
        break
time.sleep(0.3)


# select another
driver.find_element_by_xpath(select2_multi_container_xpath).click()
available_items = driver.find_elements_by_xpath("//ul[@id='select2-country_m\
ultiple-results']/li")
for x in available_items:
    if x.text == "United Kingdom":
        x.click()
        break
```

To deselect an option is to click the little 'x' on the right. In fact, it is the idea to clear all selections first then select the wanted options.

```
# clear all selections
time.sleep(0.5)
close_btns = driver.find_elements_by_xpath(select2_multi_container_xpath + "\
//span[@class='select2-selection__choice__remove']")
while(len(close_btns) > 0):
    close_btns[0].click();
    time.sleep(0.1)
    close_btns = driver.find_elements_by_xpath(select2_multi_container_xpath\
 + "//span[@class='select2-selection__choice__remove']")
```

Some might say the test scripts are quite complex. That's good thinking, if many of our test steps are written like this, it will be quite hard to maintain. One common way is to extract them into reusable functions, like below:

```
def select2_multiple_clear(self, select_id):
    select2_multi_container_xpath = "//select[@id='" + select_id + "']/../sp\
an[contains(@class, 'select2-container')]"
    close_btns = driver.find_elements_by_xpath(select2_multi_container_xpath\
 + "//span[@class='select2-selection__choice__remove']")
    flag_cleared = 0
    while (len(close_btns) > 0):
        close_btns[0].click();
        time.sleep(0.1)
        flag_cleared = 1
        close_btns = driver.find_elements_by_xpath(select2_multi_container_x\
path + "//span[@class='select2-selection__choice__remove']")
    if flag_cleared == 1:
        driver.find_element_by_xpath(select2_multi_container_xpath).click()

def select2_multiple_select(self, select_id, option_label):
    select2_multi_container_xpath = "//select[@id='" + select_id + "']/../sp\
an[contains(@class, 'select2-container')]"
    driver.find_element_by_xpath(select2_multi_container_xpath).click()
    available_items = driver.find_elements_by_xpath("//ul[@id='select2-count\
ry_multiple-results']/li")
    for x in available_items:
        if x.text == option_label:
            x.click()
```

```
        break

#  ...

def test_wrap_chosen_in_reusable_functions(self):
    #  ... land to the page with a select2 list
    self.select2_multiple_select("country_multiple", "United States")
    self.select2_multiple_select("country_multiple", "Australia")
    self.select2_multiple_clear("country_multiple")
    self.select2_multiple_select("country_multiple", "United Kingdom")
```

You can find more techniques for writing maintainable tests from my other book *Practical Web Test Automation*[2].

18.8 AngularJS web pages

AngularJS is a popular client-side JavaScript framework that can be used to extend HTML. Here is a web page (simple TODO list) developed in AngularJS.

1 of 2 remaining [archive]

- ☑ learn angular
- ☐ build an angular app

[add new todo here] [add]

HTML Source

The page source (via "View Page Source" in browser) is different from what you saw on the page. It contains some kind of dynamic coding (*ng-xxx*).

---

[2]https://leanpub.com/practical-web-test-automation

```
<div ng-controller="TodoCtrl">
  <span>{{remaining()}} of {{todos.length}} remaining</span>
  [ <a href="" ng-click="archive()">archive</a> ]
  <ul class="unstyled">
    <li ng-repeat="todo in todos">
      <input type="checkbox" ng-model="todo.done">
      <span class="done-{{todo.done}}">{{todo.text}}</span>
    </li>
  </ul>
  <form ng-submit="addTodo()">
    <input type="text" ng-model="todoText"  size="30"
           placeholder="add new todo here">
    <input class="btn-primary" type="submit" value="add">
  </form>
</div>
```

As a tester, we don't need to worry about AngularJS programming logic in the page source. To view rendered page source, which matters for testing, inspect the page via right mouse click page and select "Inspect Element".

Browser inspect view

Astute readers will notice that the 'name' attribute are missing in the input elements, replaced with 'ng-model' instead. We can use xpath to identify the web element.

The tests script below

- Add a new todo item in a text field
- Click add button
- Uncheck the 3rd todo item

```
assertIn("1 of 2 remaining", driver.page_source)
driver.find_element_by_xpath("//input[@ng-model='todoText']").send_keys("Lea\
rn test automation")
driver.find_element_by_xpath("//input[@type = 'submit' and @value='add']").c\
lick()
time.sleep(0.5)
driver.find_elements_by_xpath("//input[@type = 'checkbox' and @ng-model='tod\
o.done']")[2].click()
time.sleep(1)
assertIn("1 of 3 remaining", driver.page_source)
```

18.9 Ember JS web pages

Ember JS is another JavaScript web framework, like Angular JS, the 'Page Source' view (from browser) of a web page is raw source code, which is not useful for testing.

HTML Source

```
<div class="control-group">
  <label class="control-label" for="longitude">Longitude</label>
  <div class="controls">
    {{view Ember.TextField valueBinding="longitude"}}
  </div>
</div>
```

Browser inspect view

```
<label class="control-label" for="longitude">
    Longitude
</label>
<div class="controls">
    <input id="ember412" class="ember-view ember-text-field" type="text"></input>
</div>
```

The ID attribute of a Ember JS generated element (by default) changes. For example, this text field ID is "ember412".

Refresh the page, the ID changed to a different value.

So we shall use another way to identify the element.

```
ember_text_fields = driver.find_elements_by_xpath("//div[@class='controls']/\
input[@class='ember-view ember-text-field']")
ember_text_fields[0].send_keys("-24.0034583945")
ember_text_fields[1].send_keys("146.903459345")
ember_text_fields[2].send_keys("90%")

driver.find_element_by_xpath("//button[text() ='Update record']").click()
```

18.10 "Share Location" with Firefox

HTML5 Geolocation API can obtain a user's position. By using Geolocation API, programmers can develop web applications to provide location-aware services, such as locating the nearest restaurants. When a web page wants to use a user's location information, the user is presented with a pop up for permission.

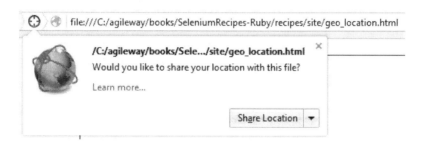

This is a native popup window, which means Selenium WebDriver cannot drive it. However, there is a workaround. We can set up a browser profile that pre-allows "Share Location" for specific websites. Here are the steps for Firefox.

1. Open Firefox with a specific profile for testing
2. Open the site
3. Type about:permissions in the address
4. Select the site and choose "Allow" option for "Share Location"

The set up and use of a specific testing profile for Firefox is already covered in Chapter 16. This only needs to be done once. After that, the test script can test location-aware web pages.

```
fp = webdriver.FirefoxProfile(get_firefox_profile_folder_by_name("testing"))
driver = webdriver.Firefox(fp)
driver.get("http://testwisely.com/demo/geo-location")
driver.find_element_by_id("use_current_location_btn").click()
time.sleep(3)
assertIn("Latitude:", driver.find_element_by_id("demo").text)
```

The method get_firefox_profile_folder_by_name is listed in Chapter 16.

18.11 Faking Geolocation with JavaScript

With Geolocation testing, it is almost certain that we will need to test the users in different locations. This can be done by JavaScript.

```
lati   = "-34.915379"  # set geo location for user
longti = "138.576777"
driver.execute_script("window.navigator.geolocation.getCurrentPosition=funct\
ion(success){; "
                      " var position = {'coords' : {'latitude': '" + lati + \
"','longitude': '" + longti + "'}}; " +
                      " success(position);}")
driver.find_element_by_id("use_current_location_btn").click()
time.sleep(1)
assertIn("-34.915379", driver.find_element_by_id("demo").text)
```

19. WYSIWYG HTML editors

WYSIWYG (an acronym for "What You See Is What You Get") HTML editors are widely used in web applications as embedded text editor nowadays. In this chapter, we will use Selenium WebDriver to test several popular WYSIWYG HTML editors.

19.1 TinyMCE

TinyMCE is a web-based WYSIWYG editor, it claims "the most used WYSIWYG editor in the world, it is used by millions"[1].

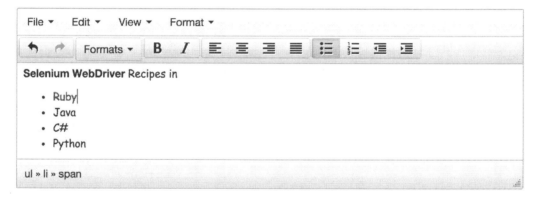

The rich text is rendered inside an inline frame within TinyMCE. To test it, we need to "switch to" that frame.

---

[1]http://www.tinymce.com/enterprise/using.php

```
driver.get("file://" + self.site_url() + "/site/tinymce-4.1.9/tinyice_demo.h\
tml")
driver.switch_to.frame("mce_0_ifr")
editor_body = driver.find_element_by_css_selector("body")
driver.execute_script("arguments[0].innerHTML = '<h1>Heading</h1> HTML'", ed\
itor_body)
time.sleep(1)
editor_body.send_keys("New content")
time.sleep(1)
editor_body.clear()

# setting html content
driver.execute_script("arguments[0].innerHTML = '<p>one</p><p>two</p>'", edi\
tor_body)

# click TinyMCE editor's 'Numbered List' button
# switch out then can drive controls on the main page
driver.switch_to.default_content()
tinymce_btn_numbered_list = driver.find_element_by_css_selector(".mce-btn[ar\
ia-label='Numbered list'] button")
tinymce_btn_numbered_list.click()

# Insert
driver.execute_script("tinyMCE.activeEditor.insertContent('<p>Brisbane</p>')\
")
```

19.2 CKEditor

CKEditor is another popular WYSIWYG editor. Like TinyMCE, CKEditor uses an inline frame.

This is some **sample text**. You are using CKEditor.

Selenium WebDriver Recipes in

- *Ruby*
- Java
- C#
- Python

```python
from selenium.webdriver.common.action_chains import ActionChains
from selenium.webdriver.common.keys import Keys

driver.get("file://" + self.site_url() + "/site/ckeditor-4.4.7/samples/uicol\
or.html")
time.sleep(1) # wait JS to load
ckeditor_frame = driver.find_element_by_class_name('cke_wysiwyg_frame')
driver.switch_to.frame(ckeditor_frame)
editor_body = driver.find_element_by_tag_name('body')
editor_body.send_keys("Selenium Recipes\n by Zhimin Zhan")
time.sleep(1)

# Clear content Another Method Using ActionBuilder to clear()
ActionChains(driver).key_down(Keys.CONTROL).send_keys("a").key_up(Keys.CONTR\
OL).perform()
ActionChains(driver).send_keys(Keys.BACK_SPACE).perform()

driver.switch_to.default_content()
# Click the numbered list button
driver.find_element_by_class_name("cke_button__numberedlist").click()
```

19.3 SummerNote

SummerNote is a Bootstrap based lightweight WYSIWYG editor, different from TinyMCE or CKEditor, it does not use frames.

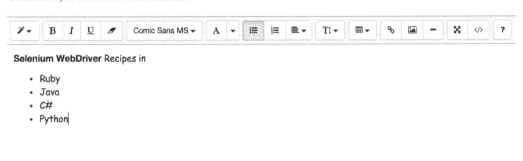

```
driver.get("file://" + self.site_url() + "/site/summernote-0.6.3/demo.html")
time.sleep(0.5)
driver.find_element_by_xpath("//div[@class='note-editor']/div[@class='note-e\
ditable']").send_keys("Text")
driver.find_element_by_xpath("//button[@data-event='insertUnorderedList']").\
click()
driver.find_element_by_xpath("//button[@data-event='codeview']").click()
driver.find_element_by_xpath("//textarea[@class='note-codable']").send_keys(\
"\n<p>HTML</p>")
```

19.4 CodeMirror

CodeMirror is a versatile text editor implemented in JavaScript. CodeMirror is not a WYSIWYG editor, but it is often used with one for editing raw HTML source for the rich text content.

```
1  <!-- write some xml below -->
2  <Selenium-WebDriverRecipes>
3    <book>in Ruby</book>
4    <book>in Java</book>
5    <book>in C#</book>
6    <book>in Python</book>
7  </
    </Selenium-WebDriverRecipes>
```

```python
from selenium.webdriver.common.action_chains import ActionChains

driver.get("file://" + self.site_url() + "/site/codemirror-5.1/demo/xmlcompl\
ete.html")
elem = driver.find_element_by_class_name("CodeMirror-scroll")
elem.click()
time.sleep(0.5)
# elem.send_keys does not work
ActionChains(driver).send_keys("<A>").perform()
```

20. Leverage Programming

The reason that Selenium WebDriver quickly overtakes other commercial testing tools (typically promoting record-n-playback), in my opinion, is embracing the programming, which offers the flexibility needed for maintainable automated test scripts.

In the chapter, I will show some examples that use some programming practices to help our testing needs.

20.1 Raise exceptions to fail test

While RSpec Expectation or MiniTest framework provides most of assertions needed, raising exceptions can be useful too as shown below.

```
import platform
print(platform.system())
if platform.system() != "Darwin":
  raise Exception("Unsupported platform: " + platform.system() )
```

In test output (when running on Windows):

```
Exception: Unsupported platform: Windows
```

An exception means an anomalous or exceptional condition occurred. The code to handle exceptions is called exception handling, an important concept in programming. If an exception is not handled, the program execution will terminate with the exception displayed.

Here is anther more complete example.

```
try:      # try block
    new_driver = webdriver.Firefox()
    new_driver.get("http://sandbox.clinicwise.net")
    new_driver.find_element_by_id("not_exists").click();
except:   # optionally: `except Exception as ex:`
    print("caught, this time I ignore")
finally:  # always get executed
    new_driver.quit()   # close the browser regardless pass or fail
```

rescue block handles the exception. If an exception is handled, the program (in our case, test execution) continues. e.backtrace returns the stack trace of the exception occurred. ensure block is always run (after) no matter exceptions are thrown (from begin) or not.

I often use exceptions in my test scripts for non-assertion purposes too.

1. Flag incomplete tests

   The problem with "TODO" comments is that you might forget them.

   ```
   def test_incomplete_test(self):
       # TO BE DONE
   ```

   I like this way better.

   ```
   def test_incomplete_test(self):
       raise Exception("To be done")
   ```

2. Stop test execution during debugging a test

   Sometimes, you want to utilize automated tests to get you to a certain page in the application quickly.

   ```
   # test steps ...
   raise Exception("Stop here, I take over from now. Delete this later.")
   # ...
   ```

20.2 Ignorable test statement error

When a test step can not be performed correctly, execution terminates and the test is marked as failed. However, failed to run certain test steps is OK sometimes. For example, we want to make sure a test starts with no active user session. If a user is currently signed in, try signing out; If a user has already signed out, performing signing out will fail. But it is acceptable.

Here is an example to capture the error/failure in a test statement (in Python), and then ignore:

```
try:
  driver.find_element_by_link_text("Sign out").click()
except:
  # ignore
```

20.3 Read external file

We can use Python's built-in file I/O (input and output) functions to read data, typically test data, from external files. Try to avoid referencing an external file using absolute path like below:

```
input_file = "C:\\temp\\in.xml" # Bad
file_content = open(input_file).read()
#  ...
```

If this test script is copied to another machine, it might fail. A common practice is to put test data with the test scripts, and refer to them using a relative path.

```
input_file = os.path.join( os.path.dirname(os.path.realpath(__file__)), "tes\
tdata", 'in.xml')
assertTrue(os.path.isfile(input_file))
file_content = open(input_file).read()
```

20.4 Data-Driven Tests with Excel

Data-Driven Testing means a test's input are driven from external sources, quite commonly in Excel or CSV files. For instance, if there is a list of user credentials with different roles and the login process is the same (but with different assertions), you can extract the test data from an excel spreadsheet and execute it one by one. Because our test scripts are in fact Python scripts, it is quite easy to do so.

A sample spreadsheet (*users.xls*) contains three username-password combination:

DESCRIPTION	LOGIN	PASSWORD	EXPECTED_TEXT
Valid Login	agileway	test	Login successful!
User name not exists	notexists	smartass	Login is not valid
Password not match	agileway	badpass	Password is not valid

The test scripts below reads the above and uses the login data to drive the browser to perform tests.

```python
import xlrd  # pip install xlrd, a library for extract data from Excel

csv_file = os.path.join( os.path.dirname(os.path.realpath(__file__)), "testd\
ata",  'users.xls')
workbook = xlrd.open_workbook(csv_file)
worksheet = workbook.sheet_by_name('users') # workbook.sheet_by_index(0)
num_rows = worksheet.nrows - 1
curr_row = -1
while curr_row < num_rows:
    curr_row += 1
    row = worksheet.row(curr_row)
    # print(row)
    login, password, expected_text = row[1].value, row[2].value, row[3].value
    if login == "LOGIN":
        continue     # ignore first head row
    driver.get("http://travel.agileway.net")
    driver.find_element_by_name("username").send_keys(login)
    driver.find_element_by_name("password").send_keys(password)
    driver.find_element_by_name("username").submit()
    assertIn(expected_text, driver.find_element_by_tag_name("body").text)
    try:
        driver.find_element_by_link_text("Sign off").click()
    except:
        # ignore
        print("Ignore if unable to sign off")
```

(The above test script requires spreadsheet gem to be installed)

20.5 Data-Driven Tests with CSV

A CSV (comma-separated values) file stores tabular data in plain-text form. CSV files are commonly used for importing into or exporting from applications. Comparing to Excel spreadsheets, a CSV file is a text file that contains only the pure data, not formatting.

The below is the CSV version of data driving test for the above user sign in example:

```
import csv

csv_file = os.path.join( os.path.dirname(os.path.realpath(__file__)), "testd\
ata", 'users.csv')
f = open(csv_file, 'rt')
try:
    reader = csv.reader(f)
    for row in reader:
        # print(row)
        login, password, expected_text = row[1], row[2], row[3]
        if login == "LOGIN":
            continue    # ignore first head row
        driver.get("http://travel.agileway.net")
        driver.find_element_by_name("username").send_keys(login)
        driver.find_element_by_name("password").send_keys(password)
        driver.find_element_by_name("username").submit()
        assertIn(expected_text, driver.find_element_by_tag_name("body").text)
        try:
            driver.find_element_by_link_text("Sign off").click()
        except:
            # ignore
            print("Ignore if unable to sign off")
finally:
    f.close
```

20.6 Identify element IDs with dynamically generated long prefixes

You can use regular expression to identify the static part of element ID or NAME. The below is a HTML fragment for a text box, we could tell some part of ID or NAME are machine generated (which might be different for next build), and the part "AppName" is meaningful.

```
<input id="ctl00_m_g_dcb0d043_e7f0_4128_99c6_71c113f45dd8_ctl00_tAppName_I"
   name="ctl00$m$g_dcb0d043_e7f0_4128_99c6_71c113f45dd8$ctl00$tAppName"/>
```

If we can later verify that 'AppName' is static for each text box, the test scripts below will work. Basically it instructs Selenium to find element whose name attribute contains "tAppName" (Watir can use Regular expression directly in finder, which I think it is better).

```
driver.find_element_by_xpath("//input[contains(@name, 'AppName')]").send_key\
s("I still can")
```

20.7 Sending special keys such as Enter to an element or browser

You can use .send_keys method to send special keys (and combination) to a web control.

```
from selenium.webdriver.common.keys import Keys

elem = driver.find_element_by_id("user")
elem.clear()
elem.send_keys("agileway")
time.sleep(1) # sleep for seeing the effect

# select all (Ctrl+A) then press backspace
elem.send_keys([Keys.CONTROL, 'a'], Keys.BACK_SPACE)
time.sleep(1)
elem.send_keys("testwisely")
time.sleep(1)
elem.send_keys(Keys.ENTER) # submit the form
```

20.8 Use of unicode in test scripts

Selenium does support Unicode. Test script files containing unicode characters have to use UTF-8 encoding.

```
assertEqual(driver.find_element_by_id("unicode_test").text, "□□")
driver.find_element_by_id("user").send_keys("проворный")
```

20.9 Extract a group of dynamic data : verify search results in order

The below is a sortable table, i.e., users can sort table columns in ascending or descending order by clicking the header.

Product ▲	Released	URL
BuildWise	2010	https://testwisely.com/buildwise
ClinicWise	2013	https://clinicwise.net
SiteWise CMS	2014	http://sitewisecms.com
TestWise	2007	https://testwisely.com/testwise

To verify sorting, we need to extract all the data in the sorted column then verify the data in desired order. Knowledge of coding with List or Array is required.

```
driver.find_element_by_id("heading_product").click()  # first asc
first_cells = driver.find_elements_by_xpath("//tbody/tr/td[1]")
product_names = [v.text for v in first_cells]
# print(product_names);
assertEqual(product_names, sorted(product_names))

driver.find_element_by_id("heading_product").click()  # change sorting
time.sleep(1)
first_cells = driver.find_elements_by_xpath("//tbody/tr/td[1]")
product_names = [v.text for v in first_cells]
assertEqual(product_names, sorted(product_names, reverse=True))
```

This approach is not limited to data in tables. The below script extracts the scores from the elements like <span class='score'>98</span>.

```
score_elems = driver.find_elements_by_xpath("//div[@id='results']//span[@cla\
ss='score']")
# ...
```

20.10 Verify uniqueness of a set of data

Like the recipe above, extract data and store them in an array first, then compare the number of elements in the array with another one without duplicates.

```
second_cells = driver.find_elements_by_xpath("//tbody/tr/td[2]")
years_released =  [v.text for v in second_cells]
# len(set(one_list)) removes duplicates
assertEqual(len(years_released), len(list(set(years_released))))
```

20.11 Extract dynamic visible data rows from a results table

Many web search forms have filtering options that hide unwanted result entries.

Product	Released	URL	
ClinicWise	2013	https://clinicwise.net	Like
BuildWise	2010	https://testwisely.com/buildwise	Like
SiteWise CMS	2014	http://sitewisecms.com	Like
TestWise	2007	https://testwisely.com/testwise	Like
		Displaying 1 - 4 of 4	

The test scripts below verify the first product name and click the corresponding 'Like' button.

```
driver.get("file:" + site_url() + "/site/data_grid.html")
rows = driver.find_elements_by_xpath("//table[@id='grid']/tbody/tr")
self.assertEqual(4, len(rows))
first_product_name = driver.find_element_by_xpath("//table[@id='grid']//tbod\
y/tr[1]/td[1]").text
assertEqual("ClinicWise", first_product_name)
driver.find_element_by_xpath("//table[@id='grid']//tbody/tr[1]/td/button").c\
lick()
```

Now check "Test automation products only" checkbox, and only two products are shown.

```
driver.find_element_by_id("test_products_only_flag").click() # Filter results
time.sleep(0.2)
# Error: Element is not currently visible
driver.find_element_by_xpath("//table[@id='grid']//tbody/tr[1]/td/button").c\
lick()
```

The last test statement would fail with an error *Element is not currently visible*. After checking the "Test automation products only" checkbox, we see only 2 rows on screen. However, there are still 4 rows in the page, the other two are hidden.

```
▼ <tbody>
  ▶ <tr class="service_products" style="display: none;"></tr>
  ▶ <tr></tr>
  ▶ <tr class="service_products" style="display: none;"></tr>
  ▶ <tr></tr>
  </tbody>
```

The button identified by this XPath //table[@id='grid']//tbody/tr[1]/td/button is now a hidden one, therefore unable to click.

A solution is to extract the visible rows to an array, then we could check them by index.

```
displayed_rows = driver.find_elements_by_xpath("//table[@id='grid']//tbody/t\
r[not(contains(@style,'display: none'))]")
assertEqual(2, len(displayed_rows))
first_row_elem = displayed_rows[0]
new_first_product_name = first_row_elem.find_element_by_xpath("td[1]").text
assertEqual("BuildWise", new_first_product_name)
first_row_elem.find_element_by_xpath("td/button").click()
```

20.12 Extract dynamic text following a pattern using Regex

To use dynamic data created from the application, e.g. receipt number, we need to extract them out. Ideally, those data are marked by dedicated IDs such as `<span id='receipt_-number'></span>`. However, it is not always the case, i.e., the data are mixed with other text.

The most commonly used approach (in programming) is to extract data with Regular Expression. Regular Expression (abbreviated *regex* or *regexp*) is a pattern of characters that finds matching text. Almost every programming language supports regular expression, with minor differences.

The test script below will extract "V7H67U" and "2015-11-9" from the text `Your coupon code: V7H67U used by 2015-11-9`, and enter the extracted coupon code in the text box.

```
driver.get("file:" + self.site_url() + "/site/coupon.html")
driver.find_element_by_id("get_coupon_btn").click()
coupon_text = driver.find_element_by_id("details").text
# Your coupon code: <b>H8ZVTA</b> used by <b>2016-2-2</b>
import re
searchObj = re.search( r'coupon code:\s+(\w+) used by\s([\d|-]+)', coupon_te\
xt, re.M|re.I)
if searchObj:
  coupon_code = searchObj.group(1)
  expiry_date = searchObj.group(2)
  print(coupon_code)
  print(expiry_date)
  driver.find_element_by_name( "coupon").send_keys(coupon_code)
else:
  raise Exception("Error: no valid coupon returned")
```

Regular expression is very powerful and it does take some time to master it. To get it going for simple text matching, however, is not hard. Google 'python regular expression' shall return some good tutorials, and Rubular[1] is a helpful tool to let you try out regular expression online.

20.13 Quick extract pattern text in comments with Regex

The way shown in previous recipe is how typical regular expression is used in coding. We can Python's Regex functions to extract pattern text in a simpler way. For example, to extract the hidden version number (in comments) on a web page like below.

```
<!-- Version: 2.19.1.9798 -->
```

Just needs one line statement.

```
re.findall(r'<!-- Version: (.*?) -->', driver.page_source)
# => ['2.19.1.9798']
```

---

[1]http://rubular.com/

re's `findall` method returns an array of matched text for a given pattern in Regex. The (.?) in the pattern is to match the text between `<!--` and `-->` as the first capturing group. If there is no match, [] is returned.

Here is a complete version of test script to verify the version number.

```
driver.get("file:" + site_url() + "/site/index.html")
import re
ver = re.findall(r'<!-- Version: (.*?) -->', driver.page_source)
print(ver)  # ['2.19.1.9798']
assertEqual(4, len(ver[0].split('.')))
assertEqual("2", ver[0].split(".")[0])   # major version
assertEqual("19", ver[0].split(".")[1])  # minor version
```

Here is another example to find multiple matches for a pattern.

```
<!-- TestWise Version: 4.7.1 -->
...
<!-- ClinicWise Version: 3.0.6 -->
```

```
app_vers = re.findall(r'<!-- (\w+) Version: (.*?) -->', driver.page_source)
print(app_vers) # [('TestWise', '4.7.1'), ('ClinicWise', '3.0.6')]
self.assertEqual("ClinicWise", app_vers[1][0])
```

21. Optimization

Working test scripts is just the first test step to successful test automation. As automated tests are executed often, and we all know the application changes frequently too. Therefore, it is important that we need our test scripts to be

- Fast
- Easy to read
- Concise

In this chapter, I will show some examples to optimize test scripts.

21.1 Assert text in page_source is faster than the text

To verify a piece of text on a web page, frequently for assertion, we can use `driver.page_-source` or `driver.find_element_by_tag_name("body").text`. Besides the obvious different output, there are big performance differences too. To get a text view (for a whole page or a web control), Webdriver needs to analyse the raw HTML to generate the text view, and it takes time. We usually do not notice that time when the raw HTML is small. However, for a large web page like the WebDriver standard[1] (over 430KB in file size), incorrect use of 'text view' will slow your test execution significantly.

```
import time
driver.get("file:" + site_url() + "/site/WebDriverStandard.html")
start_time = time.time()
assertIn("language-neutral wire protocol", driver.find_element_by_tag_name("\
body").text)
print("Method 1: Search whole document text took ", time.time() - start_time\
, " seconds")

start_time = time.time()
```

---

[1] http://www.w3.org/TR/webdriver/

```
assertIn("language-neutral wire protocol", driver.page_source)
print("Method 2: Search whole document HTML took ", time.time() - start_time\
, " seconds")
```

Let's see the difference.

```
Method 1: Search page text took 3.38 seconds
Method 2: Search page HTML took 0.09 seconds
```

21.2 Getting text from more specific element is faster

A rule of thumb is that we save execution time by narrowing down a more specific control. The two assertion statements largely achieve the same purpose but with big difference in execution time.

```
assertIn("language-neutral wire protocol", driver.find_element_by_tag_name("\
body").text)
```

Execution time: **3.39** seconds

```
assertIn("language-neutral wire protocol", driver.find_element_by_id("abstra\
ct").text)
```

Execution time: **0.05** seconds

21.3 Avoid programming if-else block code if possible

It is common that programmers write test scripts in a similar way as coding applications, while I cannot say it is wrong. For me, I prefer simple, concise and easy to read test scripts. Whenever possible, I prefer one line of test statement matching one user operation. This can be quite helpful when debugging test scripts. For example, By using ternary operator ? :, the below 4 lines of test statements

```
if "VIP" in ref_no: # Special Guest
  assertEqual("Please go upstairs", driver.find_element_by_id("notes").text)
else:
  assertEqual("", driver.find_element_by_id("notes").text)
```

is reduced to one.

```
assertEqual("Please go upstairs" if "VIP" in ref_no else "", driver.find_ele\
ment_by_id("notes").text)
```

21.4 Use variable to cache not-changed data

Commonly, I saw people wrote tests like the below to check multiple texts on a page.

```
driver.get("file:" + site_url() + "/site/WebDriverStandard.html")
assertIn("Firefox", driver.find_element_by_tag_name("body").text)
assertIn("chrome", driver.find_element_by_tag_name("body").text)
assertIn("W3C", driver.find_element_by_tag_name("body").text)
```

Execution time: **10.1** seconds

The above three test statements are very inefficient, as every test statement calls `driver.find_element_by_tag_name("body").text`, this can be a quite expensive operation when a web page is large.

Solution: use a variable to store the text (view) of the web page, a very common practice in programming.

```
the_page_text = driver.find_element_by_tag_name("body").text
assertIn("Firefox", the_page_text)
assertIn("chrome", the_page_text)
assertIn("W3C", the_page_text)
```

Execution time: **3.5** seconds

As you can see, we get quite constant execution time no matter how many assertions we perform on that page, as long as the page text we are checking is not changing.

21.5 Enter large text into a text box

We commonly use send_keys to enter text into a text box. When the text string you want
to enter is quite large, e.g. thousands of characters, try to avoid using send_keys, as it is not
efficient. Here is an example.

```
long_str = "START" + '0' * 1024 * 5  + "END" # just over 5K
text_area_elem = driver.find_element_by_id("comments")
text_area_elem.send_keys(long_str)
```

Execution time: **11.1** seconds.

When this test is executed in Chrome, you can see a batch of text 'typed' into the text box.
Furthermore, there might be a limited number of characters that WebDriver 'send' into a text
box for browsers at one time. I have seen test scripts that broke long text into trunks and then
sent them one by one, not elegant.

The **solution** is actually quite simple: using JavaScript.

```
driver.execute_script("document.getElementById('comments').value = arguments\
[0];", long_str)
```

Execution time: **0.01** seconds

21.6 Use Environment Variables to change test behaviours dynamically

Typically, there are more than one test environment we need to run automated tests against,
and we might want to run the same test in different browsers now and then. I saw the test
scripts like the below often in projects.

```
TARGET_SITE_URL = "https://physio.clinicwise.net"
# TARGET_SITE_URL = "https://yake.clinicwise.net"
TARGET_BROWSER = "chrome"
# TARGET_BROWSER = "firefox"

def tearDown(self):
    self.driver.quit()

def test_change_browser_or_url_by_updating_constants(self):
    if self.TARGET_BROWSER == "chrome":
      self.driver = webdriver.Chrome()
    else:
      self.driver = webdriver.Firefox()
    self.driver.get(self.TARGET_SITE_URL)
```

It works like this: testers comment and uncomment a set of test statements to let test script run against different servers in different browsers. This is not an ideal approach, because it is inefficient, error prone and introducing unnecessary check-ins (changing test script files with no changes to testing logic).

A simple solution is to use agreed environment variables, so that the target server URL and browser type can be set externally, outside the test scripts.

```
site_url = os.environ.get("TARGET_SITE_URL", "https://physio.clinicwise.net")
browser = os.environ.get("BROWSER", "chrome") # if not defined, use "chrome"
if browser == "firefox":
  self.driver = webdriver.Firefox()
else:
  self.driver = webdriver.Chrome()
self.driver.get(site_url)
```

For example, to run this test against another server in Chrome on Windows, run below commands.

```
> set TARGET_BROWSER=chrome
> set SITE_URL=http://yake.clinicwise.net
> py your_test.py
```

This approach is commonly used in Continuous Testing process.

21.7 Test web site in two languages

The test scripts below to test user authentication for two test sites, the same application in two languages: *http://physio.clinicwise.net* in English and *http://yake.clinicwise.net* in Chinese. While the business features are the same, the text shown on two sites are different, so are the test user accounts.

```
site_url = os.environ.get("TARGET_SITE_URL", "https://physio.clinicwise.net")
self.driver.get(site_url)
if "physio" in site_url :
  driver.find_element_by_id("username").send_keys("natalie")
  driver.find_element_by_id("password").send_keys("test")
  driver.find_element_by_id("signin_button").click()
  assertIn("Signed in successfully.", driver.page_source)
else:
  driver.find_element_by_id("username").send_keys("tuo")
  driver.find_element_by_id("password").send_keys("test")
  driver.find_element_by_id("signin_button").click()
  assertIn("□□□□", driver.page_source)
```

Though the above test scripts work, it seems lengthy and repetitive.

```
def is_chinese(self):
  return "yake" in self.site_url

def test_two_languages_with_tenary_operator(self):
  self.driver = webdriver.Chrome()
  self.site_url = os.environ.get("TARGET_SITE_URL", "https://physio.clinicwi\
se.net")
  self.driver.get(self.site_url)
  self.driver.find_element_by_id("username").send_keys("tuo" if self.is_chin\
ese() else "natalie")
  self.driver.find_element_by_id("password").send_keys("test")
  self.driver.find_element_by_id("signin_button").click()
  self.assertIn("□□□□" if self.is_chinese() else "Signed in successfully.", \
self.driver.page_source)
```

Using IDs can greatly save multi-language testing

When doing multi-language testing, try not to use the actual text on the page for non user-entering operations. For example, the test statements are not optimal.

```
driver.find_element_by_link_text("Register").click()
# or below with some programming logic ...
driver.find_element_by_link_text("Registre").click() # french
driver.find_element_by_link_text("□□").click()        # chinese
```

Using IDs is much simpler.

```
driver.find_element_by_id("register_link").click()
```

This works for all languages.

21.8 Multi-language testing with lookups

We can extend the approach used in previous recipe (if-elif-elif-else) to work with multiple languages.

```
# return the current language used on the site
def site_lang(self):
  # ... may use self.site_url to determine
  if "yake" in self.site_url:
      return "chinese"
  elif "dentaire" in self.site_url:
      return "french"
  else:
      return "english"


def test_multiple_languages_1(self):
  self.driver = webdriver.Chrome()
  self.site_url = os.environ.get("TARGET_SITE_URL", "https://physio.clinicwi\
se.net")
  self.driver.get(self.site_url)

  # return the current language used on the site
  if self.site_lang() == "chinese":
    self.driver.find_element_by_id("username").send_keys("hongyu")
  elif self.site_lang() == "french":
    self.driver.find_element_by_id("username").send_keys("dupont")
  else:  # default to english
    self.driver.find_element_by_id("username").send_keys("natalie")
```

If this is going to be used only once, the above is fine. However, these login test steps will be used heavily, which will lead to lengthy and hard to maintain test scripts.

Solution: centralize the logic with lookups.

```
def user_lookup(self, username):
  if self.site_lang() == "chinese":
      return "hongyu"
  elif self.site_lang() == "french":
      return "dupont"
  else:
      return "natalie"


# in test case
```

```
self.driver.find_element_by_id("username").send_keys(self.user_lookup("natal\
ie"))
```

Astute readers may point out, "You over-simplify the cases, there surely will be more test users." Yes, that's true. I was trying to the simplest way to convey the lookup.

```
def setUp(self):
  natalie_logins = { "english": "natalie", "french": "dupont", "chinese": "\
hongyu"}
  mark_logins = { "english": "mark", "french": "marc", "chinese": "li"}
  self.user_lookups = {
    'natalie': natalie_logins,
    'mark':  mark_logins
  }

def user_lookup(self, username):
  return self.user_lookups[username][self.site_lang()]
```

In summary, the test user in a chosen language (English in above example) is used as the key to look up for other languages. The equivalent user of "natalie" in French is "dupont".

Some, typically programmers, write the test scripts like the below.

```
def get_admin_user(self):
  # logic goes here
  return "..."

# in test case
self.driver.find_element_by_id("username").send_keys(self.get_admin_user())
```

If there are only a handful users, it may be OK. But I often see hard-to-read test statements such as get_register_user_1() and get_manager_2(). I cannot say this approach is wrong, I just prefer using 'personas'. But I am against reading test users from external configuration files, which generally I found, hard to maintain.

22. Gotchas

For the most part, Selenium WebDriver API is quite straightforward. My one sentence summary: find a element and perform an operation on it. Writing test scripts in Selenium WebDriver is much more than knowing the API, it involves programming, HTML, JavaScript and web browsers. There are cases that can be confusing to newcomers.

22.1 Test starts browser but no execution with blank screen

A very possible cause is that the version of installed Selenium WebDriver is not compatible with the version of your browser. Here is a screenshot of Firefox 41.0.2 started by a Selenium WebDriver 2.44.0 test.

The test hung there. After I upgraded Selenium WebDriver to 2.45, the test ran fine.

This can happen to Chrome too. With both browsers and Selenium WebDriver get updated quite frequently, in a matter of months, it is not that surprising to get the incompatibility issues. For test engineers who are not aware of this, it can be quite confusing as the tests might be running fine the day before and no changes have been made since.

Once knowing the cause, the solutions are easy:

- Upgrade both Selenium WebDriver and browsers to the latest version

  Browsers such as Chrome usually turn on auto-upgrade by default, I suggest upgrading to the latest Selenium WebDriver several days after it is released.
- Lock Selenium Webdriver and browsers.

  Turn off auto-upgrade in browser and be thoughtful on upgrading Selenium Webdriver.

Be aware of browser and driver changes

One day I found over 40 test failures (out of about 400) by surprise on the latest continuous testing build. There were little changes since the last build, in which all tests passed. I quickly figured out the cause: Chrome auto-upgraded to v44. Chrome 44 with the ChromeDriver 2.17 changed the behaviour of clicking hyperlinks. After clicking a link, sometimes test executions immediately continue to the next operation without waiting for the "clicking link" operation to finish.

```
driver.find_element_by_id("new_client").click()
time.sleep(0.5) # hack for chrome v44, make sure the link is clicked
```

A week later, I noticed the only line in the change log of ChromeDriver v2.18:

```
"Changes include many bug fixes that allow ChromeDriver to work more reliabl\
y with Chrome 44+."
```

22.2 Failed to assert copied text in browser

To answer this, let's start with an example. What we see in a browser (Internet Explorer)

BOLD *Italic*

```
Text assertion
(new line before)!
```

is the result of rendering the page source (HTML) below in Internet Explorer:

```
<p id="text"> <b>BOLD</b> <i>Italic<i> </p>
<pre id="formatted">Text assertion  
(new line before)!</pre>
```

As you can see, there are differences. Test scripts can be written to check the text view (what we saw) on browsers or its raw page source (HTML). To complicate things a little more, old versions of browsers may return slightly different results.

Don't worry. As long as you understand the text shown in browsers are coming from raw HTML source, after a few attempts, this is usually not a problem. Here are the test scripts for checking text and source for above example:

```
# tags in source not in text
assertIn("BOLD Italic", driver.find_element_by_tag_name("body").text)
assertIn("<b>BOLD</b>  <i>Italic</i>",driver.page_source)

# HTML entities in source but shown as space in text
assertIn("assertion  \n(new line before)", driver.find_element_by_tag_name("\
body").text)

# note the second character after assertion is non-breaable space ( )
if driver.capabilities["browserName"] == "firefox":
    # different behaviour on Firefox (v25)
    assertIn("assertion  \n(new line before)", driver.page_source)
else:
    assertIn("assertion  \n(new line before)", driver.page_source)
```

22.3 The same test works for Chrome, but not for IE

Chrome, Firefox and IE are different products and web browsers are very complex software. Comparing to other testing frameworks, Selenium WebDriver provides better support for all major browsers. Still there will be some operations work differently on one than another.

```
browser_name = driver.capabilities["browserName"]
print(browser_name)
if browser_name == "firefox":
    # firefox specific test statement
elif browser_name == "chrome":
    # chrome specific test statement
else:
    raise Exception("unsupported browser: " + browser_name)
```

Some might say that it will require a lot of work. Yes, cross-browser testing is associated with more testing effort, obviously. However, from my observation, few IT managers acknowledge this. That's why cross-testing is talked a lot, but rarely gets done.

22.4 "unexpected tag name 'input'"

This is because there is another control matching your find_element and it is a different control type (input tag). For example,

```
<input type="checkbox" name="vip" value="on"> VIP?

<!-- ... -->
<select name="vip"/>
  <option value="true">Yes</option>
  <option value="false">No/option>
</select>
```

The intention of the test script below's intention is to select 'Yes' in the dropdown list, but not aware of there is another checkbox control sharing exactly the same name attribute.

```
from selenium.webdriver.support.ui import Select
#...
Select(driver.find_element_by_name("vip")).select_by_visible_text("No")
```

Here is the error returned:

```
'ArgumentError: unexpected tag name "input"'
```

The solution is quite obvious after knowing the cause: change the locator to ' Select(driver.find_-element_by_xpath("//select[@name='vip']")).select_by_visible_text("No")'.

A quite common scenario is as below: a hidden element and a checkbox element share the same ID and NAME attributes.

```
<input type="hidden" name="vip" value="false"/>
<!-- ... -->
<input type="checkbox" name="vip" value="on"> VIP?
```

In this case, there might be no error thrown. However, this can be more subtle, as the operation is applied to a different control.

22.5 Element is not clickable or not visible

Some controls such as textfields, even when they are not visible in the current browser window, Selenium WebDriver will move the focus to them. Some other controls such as buttons, may be not. In that case, though the element is found by `find_element`, it is not clickable.

The solution is to make the target control visible in browser.

1. Scroll the window to make the control visible

   Find out the control's position and scroll to it.

   ```
   elem = driver.find_element_by_name("submit_action_2")
   elem_pos = elem.location["y"]
   driver.execute_script("window.scroll(0, {})".format(elem_pos))
   ```

   Or scroll to the top / bottom of page.

   ```
   driver.execute_script("window.scrollTo(0, document.body.scrollHeight);")
   ```

2. A hack, call `send_keys` to a text field nearby, if there is one.

23. Selenium Remote Control Server

Selenium Server, formerly known as Selenium Remote Control (RC) Server, allows testers to writes Selenium tests in their favourite language and execute them on another machine. The word 'remote' means that the test scripts and the target browser may not be on the same machine.

The Selenium Server is composed of two pieces: a server and a client.

- **Selenium Server**. A Java server which automatically launches, drives and kills browsers, with the target browser installed on the machine.
- **Client libraries**. Test scripts in tests' favourite language bindings, such as Ruby, Java and Python.

23.1 Selenium Server Installation

Make sure you have Java Runtime installed first. Download Selenium Server *selenium-server-standalone-{VERSION}.jar* from Selenium download page[1] and place it on the computer with the browser you want to test on. Then from the directory with the jar run the following from Command Line

```
java -jar selenium-server-standalone-2.53.1.jar
```

Sample output

---

[1]http://www.seleniumhq.org/download/

```
09:34:41.616 INFO - Launching a standalone Selenium Server
09:34:41.747 INFO - Java: Oracle Corporation 25.77-b03
09:34:41.747 INFO - OS: Mac OS X 10.11.5 x86_64
09:34:41.778 INFO - v2.53.1, with Core v2.53.1. Built from revision a36b8b1
...
09:37:43.973 INFO - RemoteWebDriver instances should connect to: http://127.\
0.0.1:4444/wd/hub
09:37:43.973 INFO - Selenium Server is up and running
```

There are two options you can pass to the server: timeout and browserTimeout.

```
java -jar selenium-server-standalone-2.53.1.jar -timeout=20 -browserTimeout=\
60
```

23.2 Execute tests in specified browser on another machine

Prerequisites:

- Make sure the Selenium Server is up and running.
- You can connect to the server via HTTP.
- Note down the server machine's IP address.

To change existing local Selenium tests (running on a local browser) to remote Selenium tests (running on a remote browser) is very easy, just update the initalization of Selenium::WebDriver as below:

```
driver = webdriver.Remote(desired_capabilities={
        "browserName": "firefox",
    })
driver.get("http://travel.agileway.net")
# ...
```

The test scripts (client) is expected to terminate each browser session properly, calling `driver.quit`.

Of course, we can specify a different browser as long as it is installed and configured properly, on the remote server.

```
driver = webdriver.Remote(
        command_executor = 'http://127.0.0.1:4444/wd/hub',
        desired_capabilities = { "browserName": "chrome" }
    )
```

23.3 Selenium Grid

Selenium Grid allows you to run Selenium tests in parallel to cut down the execution time. Selenium Grid includes one hub and many nodes.

1. **Start the Hub**

   The hub receives the test requests and distributes them to the nodes.

   ```
   java -jar selenium-server-standalone-2.53.1.jar -role hub
   ```

2. **Start the nodes**

   A node gets tests from the hub and run them.

   ```
   java -jar selenium-server-standalone-2.53.1.jar -role node  -hub http://loca\
   lhost:4444/grid/register
   ```

   If you starts a node on another machine, replace *localhost* with the hub's IP address.

3. **Using grid to run tests**

   You need to change the test script to point to the driver to the hub.

   ```
   driver = webdriver.Remote(desired_capabilities={
           "browserName": "chrome",
           })
   # ...
   ```

The usual way to run test from the command line:

```
> pyhton -m unittest agile_travel_test.py
Ran 1 test in 8.320s
```

```
OK
```

The test will run on one of the nodes. Please note that the timing and test case counts (from RSpec) returned is apparently not right.

Frankly, I haven't yet met anyone who is able to show me a working selenium-grid running a fair number of UI selenium tests.

Here are my concerns with Selenium Grid:

- **Complexity**

  For every selenium grid node, you need to configure the node either by specifying command line parameters or a JSON file. Check out the Grid Wiki page[2] for details.

  It is my understanding that just pushing the tests to the hub, and it handles the rest based on the configuration. My experience tells me that it is too good to be true. For example, here is an error I got. While the error message is quite clear: no ChromeDriver installed. But on which node? Shouldn't the hub 'know' about that?

  ```
  [remote server] com.google.common.base.Preconditions(Preconditions.java):177\
  :in `checkState': The path to the driver executable must be set by the webdr\
  iver.chrome.driver system property; for more information, see http://code.go\
  ogle.com/p/selenium/wiki/ChromeDriver. The latest version can be downloaded \
  from http://chromedriver.storage.googleapis.com/index.html (java.lang.Illega\
  lStateException) (Selenium::WebDriver::Error::UnknownError)
  ```

- **Very limited control**

  Selenium-Grid comes with a web accessible console, in my view, very basic one. For instance, I created 2 nodes: one on Mac; the other on Windows 7 (the console displayed as 'VISTA').

---

[2]https://code.google.com/p/selenium/wiki/Grid2

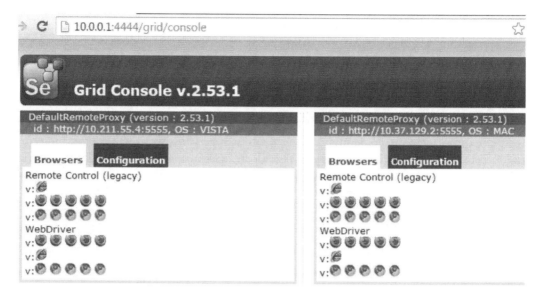

An IE icon for for Mac node? This does not seem right.

- **Lack of feedback**

  UI tests take time to execute, more tests means longer execution time. Selenium Grid's distribution model is to reduce that. Apart from the raw execution time, there is also the feedback time. The team would like to see the test results as soon as a test execution finishes on one node. Even better, when we pass the whole test suite to the hub, it will 'intelligently' run new or last failed tests first. Selenium Grid, in my view, falls short on this.

- **Lack of rerun**

  In a perfect world, all tests execute as expected every single time. But in reality, there are so many factors that could affect the test execution:
    - test statements didn't wait long enough for AJAX requests to complete (server on load)
    - browser crashes (it happens)
    - node runs out of disk space
    - virus scanning process started in background
    - windows self-installed an update
    - ...
  In this case, re-assign failed tests to anther node could save a potential good build.

My point is: I could quickly put together a demo with Selenium Grid running tests on different nodes (with different browsers), and the audience might be quite impressed. However, in reality, when you have a large number of UI test suites, the game is totally different. The whole process needs to be simple, stable, flexible and very importantly, being able to provide feedback quickly. In the true spirit of Agile, if there are tests failing, no code shall be allowed to check in. Now we are talking about the pressure ...

How to achieve distributed test execution over multiple browsers? First of all, distributed test execution and cross browser testing are two different things. Distributed test execution speeds up test execution (could be just against single type of browser); while cross-browser testing is to verify the application's ability to work on a range of browsers. Yes, distributed test execution can be used to test against different browsers. But do get distributed test execution done solidly before worrying about the cross browser testing.

I firmly believe the UI test execution with feedback shall be a part of continuous integration (CI) process, just like running xUnit tests and the report shown on the CI server. It is OK for developers/testers to develop selenium tests in an IDE, in which they run one or a handful tests often. However, executing a large number of UI tests, which is time consuming, shall be done in the CI server.

The purpose of a prefect CI process: building the application to pass all tests, to be ready to production release. Distributed execution of UI tests with quick feedback, in my opinion, is an important feature of a CI Server. However, most CI servers in the market do not support this feature. You can find more information on this topic in my other book *Practical Web Test Automation*[3].

---

[3]https://leanpub.com/practical-web-test-automation

Appendix - Continuous Testing

This book shows recipes on solving individual test scenarios with Selenium WebDriver. Ideally, we run all the test scripts to verify every new build as regression testing. However, when total execution time of all tests exceeds one hour, it is becoming impractical to run them often on testers' machines. The solution is to execute tests in Continuous Testing server.

Obviously continuous testing is a big topic, here I will just cover a bare minimum to show you one approach to run a suite of Selenium (in Python) test scripts with a click of a button.

Set up BuildWise Server

BuildWise is a continous testing server for easier executing automated UI tests. BuildWise is free and open-source, and runs on Windows, Mac OS X and Linux.

Prerequisite

The very first step of CI build is to check out code or scripts from a source control system, such as Git. If you haven't got your test scripts in a source control, I recommend to use Git. It is quite easy to do set up, and there are plenty Git tutorials you can find online.

In the exercise, I will use one sample Git repository on GitHub[4]. The folder containing Selenium Python test scripts is `selenium-webdriver-python-unittest`.

Installation

- **Ruby**

  BuildWise requires Ruby to run. Follow the standard process to install Ruby for your operating system:
    - Windows: Ruby Installer[5]
    - Mac OS X: No need, it already included.
    - Linux: usually one command to install with the package manager.

---

[4]https://github.com/testwisely/agiletravel-ui-tests
[5]https://rubyinstaller.org/

If your are going to install BuildWise on Windows, I strongly recommend to download and install RubyShell[6], a packaged installer of standard Ruby for Windows and all required libraries (called Gems in Ruby) for BuildWise.

- **MySQL database** (free Community Edition)

The database for storing build results. Download and install MySQL Community Server[7] for your OS.

- **BuildWise Server**

Download BuildWise server (in a zip file) from the book site[8]. Unzip it to a folder, e.g. c:\agileway\buildwise-1.7.0).

- **Install required Ruby gems**

You may skip this step if using RubyShell. Otherwise, follow the ReadMe.txt to install all the gems.

Configuration

- **Create database for BuildWise**

```
> mysqladmin -u root -p  create buildwise_production
```

- **Verify Database Configuration**

Open the database configuration file C:\agileway\buildwise-1.7.0\config\database.yml (assuming installed under *c:\agileway\buildwise-1.7.0*).

```
production:
  adapter: mysql2
  encoding: utf8
  database: buildwise_production
  host: 127.0.0.1
  pool: 10
  username: root
  password: buildwise
```

Update the configuration if necessary.

---

[6]http://testwisely.com/testwise/downloads
[7]http://dev.mysql.com/downloads/mysql/
[8]http://zhimin.com/books/selenium-recipes-python

Start BuildWise Server

Run `startup.bat` or `startup.sh` to start the BuildWise server. Open `http://localhost:3618` in your browser. If you see this:

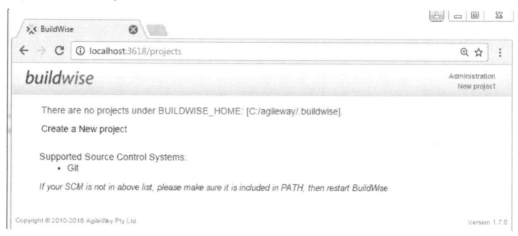

Congratulations, BuildWise is up and running.

Verify build server machine can run Selenium Python

Before we start running Selenium python tests in BuildWise server, it is a good idea to make sure we can run selenium tests from command line on this build server machine.

1. Install Python3

   Download Python 3[9] and run the installer. Make sure ticking the "Add python.exe to Path" checkbox on installation.

2. Install Selenium and required libraries

   ~~~> pip3 install selenium > pip3 install pytest~~

   pytest[10] is a Python testing tool. The reason we use pytest here is to run unittest style tests with JUnit style reports.

3. Verify that you can run Selenium Python tests on the build server machine

   cd temp git clone https://github.com/testwisely/agiletravel-ui-tests cd agiletravel-ui-tests\selenium-webdriver-python-unittest\test pytest login_test.py

---

[9]https://www.python.org/downloads
[10]http://docs.pytest.org/en/latest/

Create Build Project in BuildWise

Click "New project" link on the BuildWise server (in browser). Fill the form as below:

New project

Option 1. Loading from a working folder or Specify manually

Name:	AgileTravel Quick Build Python Unittest
Identifier:	agiletravel-quick-build-python-unittest
	(lower case and unique, e.g. adminwise-ui-tests)
Working folder:	C:/temp/agiletravel-ui-tests
	(Specify the SCM checked out project folder on the machine running BuildWise server, e.g. c:\git\myworkdir)
SCM Login:	username	password
	(You may want to use dedicated user for CI, if you have set up SSH without login or embed user:password in Git)
Project Template:	Continuous Test Server
UI test folder:	selenium-webdriver-python-unittest/test
	(where the UI tests are, relative to project root directory, eg. **spec** *or* **ui-tests/spec***)*
Rake Task for UI Tests:	-f selenium-webdriver-python-unittest/Rakefile ui_tests:quick
	(e.g. **ci:ui_tests:full***. You may configure this later.)*

[Create] [Cancel]

Click "Create" button.

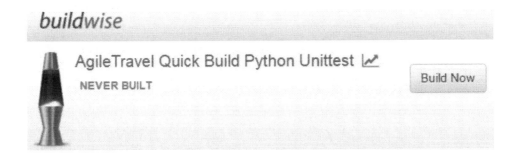

buildwise

AgileTravel Quick Build Python Unittest 📈

NEVER BUILT

[Build Now]

Execute test sequentially on Build Server

Click "Build Now" button to kick of an execution of all tests in BuildWise.

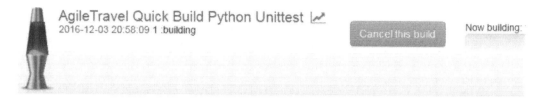

To include or exclude specific test scripts files for the build, edit Rakefile. **Rakefile** is the configuration file for Rake, the default task management tool for Ruby. You do need basic Ruby language knowledge to customise the tasks defined in Rakefile.

View test report

You can click the build to see the build output in progress. A test report will be present when test execution completes. Here is an sample with one out of five test failed.

1
errors

Administration
New project

AgileTravel Quick Build Python Unittest   Build #14 Failed

Started at: **2016-12-04 18:58**   Finished at: **2016-12-04 18:59**   Duration: **1 minute**

▶ Change log
▶ Build artifacts
▼ UI Test Results (5 test cases) | Export 🗷 Excel , CSV

TEST FILE (5 test cases in 1 test scripts files)	TIME (S)	RESULTS ▲
TEST-SUITE.xml 🗐	64.6	
- test_select_flight	13.8	OK
- test_sign_in_failed	7.6	Failure
- test_sign_in_ok	5.1	OK
- test_enter_passenger_details	15.2	OK
- test_payment_by_credit_card	21.8	OK

Afterword

First of all, if you haven't downloaded the recipe test scripts from the book site[11], I strongly recommend you to do so. It is free for readers who have purchased the ebook through Leanpub.

This book comes with two formats: *Ebook* and *Paper book*. I originally thought there won't be much demand for printed book, as the convenient 'search ability' of ebooks is good for this kind of solution books. However, during on-site consultation, I found testers I worked with kept borrowing my printed proof-copy and wanted to buy it. It's why I released the paper book on Amazon[12] as well.

Practice makes perfect

Like any other skills, you will get better at it by practising more.

- **Write tests**

  Many testers would like to practise test automation with Selenium WebDriver, but they don't have a good target application to write tests against. Here I make one of my applications available for you: ClinicWise sandbox site[13]. ClinicWise is a modern web application using popular web technologies such as AJAX and Bootstrap. I have written 576 Selenium WebDriver tests for ClinicWise. Execution of all tests takes more than 4 hours on a single machine. If you like, you can certainly practise writing tests against ClinicWise sandbox.

  ClinicWise is also a show case of web applications designed for testing, which means it is easier to write automated tests against it. Our every Selenium test starts with calling a database reset: visit *http:///sandbox.clinicwise.net/reset*, which will reset the database to a seeded state.

---

[11]http://zhimin.com/books/selenium-recipes-python
[12]https://www.amazon.com/Selenium-WebDriver-Recipes-Python-problem/dp/1514256576
[13]http:///sandbox.clinicwise.net

Wise Clinic sandbox

Database is reset. Current access token expires in 30 minutes   ×

| User name | Password | Sign in |

Forgot password?

User Logins (passwords: *test*)

Admin: admin
Therapists: mark*, jackie, tom
Receptions: natalie
Nurse: sharon

- **Improve programming skills**

  It requires programming skills to effectively use Selenium WebDriver. For readers with no programming background, the good news is that the programming knowledge required for writing test scripts is much less comparing to coding applications, as you have seen in this book. If you like learning with hands-on practices, check out Learn Ruby Programming by Examples[14].

Successful Test Automation

I believe that you are well equipped to cope with most testing scenarios if you have mastered the recipes in this book. However, this only applies to your ability to write individual tests. Successful test automation also requires developing and maintaining many automated test cases while software applications change frequently.

- **Maintain test scripts to keep up with application changes**

  Let's say you have 100 automated tests that all pass. The changes developers made in the next build will affect some of your tests. As this happens too often, many automated tests will fail. The only way to keep the test script maintainable is to adopt good test design practices (such as reusable functions and page objects) and efficient refactoring. Check out my other book *Practical Web Test Automation*[15].

---

[14]https://leanpub.com/learn-ruby-programming-by-examples-en
[15]https://leanpub.com/practical-web-test-automation

- **Shorten test execution time to get quick feedback**

  With growing number of test cases, so is the test execution time. This leads to a long feedback gap from the time programmers committed the code to the time test execution completes. If programmers continue to develop new features/fixes during the gap time, it can easily get into a tail-chasing problem. This will hurt the team's productivity badly. Executing automated tests in a Continuous Testing server with various techniques (such as distributing test to run in parallel) can greatly shorten the feedback time. *Practical Web Test Automation* has one chapter on this.

Best wishes for your test automation!

Resources

Books

- **Practical Web Test Automation**[16] by Zhimin Zhan

  Solving individual selenium challenges (what this book is for) is far from achieving test automation success. *Practical Web Test Automation* is the book to guide you to the test automation success, topics include:
  - Developing easy to read and maintain Watir/Selenium tests using next-generation functional testing tool
  - Page object model
  - Functional Testing Refactorings
  - Cross-browser testing against IE, Firefox and Chrome
  - Setting up continuous testing server to manage execution of a large number of automated UI tests
  - Requirement traceability matrix
  - Strategies on team collaboration and test automation adoption in projects and organizations
- **Selenium WebDriver Recipes in Ruby**[17] by Zhimin Zhan

  Selenium WebDriver recipe tests in Ruby, another popular script language that is quite similar to Python.
- **Selenium WebDriver Recipes in Java**[18] by Zhimin Zhan

  Sometimes you might be required to write Selenium WebDriver tests in Java. Master Selenium WebDriver in Java quickly by leveraging this book.
- **Selenium WebDriver Recipes in C#, 2nd Edition**[19] by Zhimin Zhan

  Selenium WebDriver recipe tests in C#, another popular language that is quite similar to Java.

---

[16]https://leanpub.com/practical-web-test-automation
[17]https://leanpub.com/selenium-recipes-in-ruby
[18]https://leanpub.com/selenium-recipes-in-java
[19]http://www.apress.com/9781484217412

- **Selenium WebDriver Recipes in Node.js**[20] by Zhimin Zhan

  Selenium WebDriver recipe tests in Node.js, a very fast implementation of WebDriver in JavaScript.
- **API Testing Recipes in Ruby**[21] by Zhimin Zhan

  The problem solving guide to testing APIs such as SOAP and REST web services in Ruby language.

Web Sites

- **Selenium Python API**[22]

  The API has searchable interface, The *Locators* and *Element* class are particularly important:
    - Locate elements By[23]
    - Element[24]
- **Python unitest**[25]

  Python's unit testing framework.
- **Selenium Home** (http://seleniumhq.org[26])

Tools

- **PyCharm**[27]

  Python IDE from JetBrains, the community edition is free.
- **BuildWise** (http://testwisely.com/buildwise[28])

  AgileWay's free and open-source continuous build server, purposely designed for running automated UI tests with quick feedback.

---

[20]https://leanpub.com/selenium-webdriver-recipes-in-nodejs

[21]https://leanpub.com/api-testing-recipes-in-ruby

[22]http://selenium-python.readthedocs.io/api.html

[23]http://selenium-python.readthedocs.io/api.html?highlight=find_element#locate-elements-by

[24]http://selenium-python.readthedocs.io/api.html#module-selenium.webdriver.remote.webelement

[25]https://docs.python.org/3/library/unittest.html

[26]http://seleniumhq.org

[27]https://www.jetbrains.com/pycharm

[28]http://testwisely.com/buildwise

Made in the USA
San Bernardino, CA
07 December 2017